THE MINIMALIST MINDSET

Danny Dover

DISCARD

Wimberley Village Library
P.O. Box 1240
Wimberley, Texas 78676

The Minimalist Mindset

Copyright © 2017 Danny Dover

All rights reserved. No parts of this publication may be reproduced, stored in a retrieval system, or transmitted in any form or by any means, electronic, mechanical, photocopying, recording, or otherwise, without the prior written permission of the copyright owner.

This book is sold subject to the condition that it shall not, by way of trade or otherwise, be lent, resold, hired out, or otherwise circulated without the publisher's prior consent in any form of binding or cover other than that in which it is published and without a similar condition including this condition being imposed on the subsequent purchaser. Under no circumstances may any part of this book be photocopied for resale.

Some names and identifying details have been changed to protect the privacy of individuals.

Disclaimer: Persons considering changing their diet or exercise regimens should consult a physician before implementing any diet or exercise program.

Intriguing Ideas Press, an imprint of Intriguing Ideas LLC
http://www.intriguingideas.com/
https://www.lifelisted.com/

ISBN-10: 0-9986467-2-5
ISBN-13: 978-0-9986467-2-5

Published in the United States of America

Version: 2.3 (P-I)

To Megan Singley. Thank you for being exactly you.

On the Shoulders of Giants

I'm merely an explorer standing on the shoulders of the giants who came before me. Though I am indebted to many people, I wish to thank this small group of special people up-front:

Adam Feldstein
Barb Dover
Craig Chelius
Ian Lauth
Jack Peterson
Jean Powell
Jeremy Ginsburg
Jessica Dover
Joe Chura
Joe Dover
Joel Runyon
Josh Dover
Megan Singley
Pat McClure
Ryan Ricketts
Sam Niccolls
The Minimalists
Tynan

Contents

Part One - A Better Way   1

Chapter 1 - The Cave   3
Chapter 2 - It Starts With a Story   9
Chapter 3 - How Does One Live Life Well?   17
Chapter 4 - Addition Isn't Possible Without Subtraction   24

Part Two - A Habit Buffet   29

Chapter 5 - All You Can Eat Habits   31
Chapter 6 - Money   34
Chapter 7 - Time   51
Chapter 8 - Work   58
Chapter 9 - Housing   69
Chapter 10 - Transportation   73
Chapter 11 - Communication   77
Chapter 12 - E-mail   83
Chapter 13 - Mobile Phone   89
Chapter 14 - Objects   94
Chapter 15 - Books   103
Chapter 16 - Photos   106
Chapter 17 - Computers   111
Chapter 18 - Clothing   117

Chapter 19 - Travel	**128**
Chapter 20 - Gifts	**135**
Chapter 21 - Food	**141**
Chapter 22 - Exercise	**151**
Chapter 23 - Friends	**160**
Chapter 24 - Significant Others	**166**
Chapter 25 - Family	**169**

Part Three - Making These Habits Your Habits — **175**

Chapter 26 - Actions	**177**
Chapter 27 - Projects	**183**
Chapter 28 - Repetition	**187**

Part Four - But Why? — **195**

Chapter 29 - Why Are You Here?	**197**
Chapter 30 - Learning From Those Who Don't Know	**200**

Additional Resources

Talking To Others About The Minimalist Mindset	**204**
Letter To Reader	**203**
About The Author	**202**

Part One: A Better Way

Chapter 1: The Cave

Learning about Plato's *Allegory of the Cave* is the perfect way to start learning about minimalism.

In Plato's *Cave* (written sometime between 380 and 360 B.C.), prisoners, imprisoned since birth, are arranged in a row with chains and rods that prevent them from ever directly seeing themselves or each other. They can talk to each other, but they cannot shift their visual perspective. Each prisoner faces the same cave wall back-lit by a fire, which showcases the shadows of everyone in the group.

Due to their forced perspective, the prisoners assume the world and themselves are composed only of the shadows and sounds that they can detect. Over time, the societal value of each of the prisoners is set by arbitrary cultural measures. In this case, the value of each prisoner is determined by the accuracy in which they can learn to identify each of the other prisoners by their shadow and voice. Since these traits are valued by the society, the more clever members of the group become the elite, and they learn to predict many of the actions that the other prisoners will take. Each day the entire world within the Cave, the ups and downs, the fights and reconciliations of all of the cave dwellers, play out on the same shadow-covered wall.

Until one day the metal constraints around one particular prisoner rusts through, and she is able to move freely. Shifting her perspective for the first time in her life, she is horrified and outraged by what she sees. She ventures out of the cave and she sees the world as it really is.

Feeling obligated to the cave dwellers, she returns to the cave to enlighten the others. In a flurry she explains to the prisoners that they are prisoners, and that the shadows are only one small piece of a much bigger world.

The elite group of the cave dwellers, who themselves are prisoners of perspective, are not pleased with the new information. They feel threatened that their generally accepted superiority may be undermined.

The woman explains that most of the world that the cave dwellers occupied was led by an elite, clever group of prisoners. Worse yet, she explains, most of the prisoners were merely observing their lives, not actually participating in them.

The reaction is almost as surprising as the revelation. The clever group of prisoners denies her new observations as heresy. Their incentives are clearly in the direction of maintaining power. The rest of the group calls her crazy and socially separates themselves from her. She offers to remove their chains, but fear and the unwillingness to take a risk causes the group to deny her. Having seen the sun, she can no longer see the shadows as clearly as she once had.

In the world that you and I live in most prisoners are not imprisoned by tangible chains, but instead by objects of their own choosing. Many people are free to travel the world or move houses, but generally choose not to out of fear of losing what possessions they have or of the effort it will require to move those possessions. Meanwhile, those same people talk online and offline about wanting to travel or fulfill their dreams, but instead fill their days working for others so that they can maintain and add to their own pile of *things*. Each day they spend money they could otherwise use to buy back their freedom. The same *things* that they showcase and protect are preventing them from escaping.

Of course real change does happen, but for some

very specific reasons, making real change is rare.

For most, the goal of life is to increase happiness. But what exactly is happiness?

Difficult questions like these are sometimes most effectively answered through indirect responses. It is for that reason that I wrote this book. This book asks about happiness but speaks about minimalism.

At a basic level, happiness is the right combination of chemicals and activated neural connections occurring within the human brain. What are the triggers for these chemicals and connections? For the most part the triggers are the things we evolved to think are good for us. This could be eating rich and sweet foods, enjoying high social status among our peers, having beneficial experiences with potential mates, and doing useful tasks like nesting, protecting, and creating things.

Historically these activities have enabled our ancestors to survive, so it is easy to understand why our brains evolved to reward us for these activities.

The problem is evolution takes a long time, and we now live in a world that is vastly unlike the world where these happiness feedback-loops developed. The reward signals that served mankind well in the past can be damaging in the world of abundance that many people live in now. (This includes those of us who have the luxuries of time and money that are required to read a book. Yes, that includes both you and me!)

The efforts and resources that are spent on earning these reward signals are similar to the efforts the prisoners expended showcasing their shadow lives. These efforts are accepted, and even encouraged, by their society, but they are not built on the foundation of a holistic perspective of the world.

Fortunately, you don't have to rebel against society and throw away all of your stuff in order to free yourself from the Cave.

In real life, the solution is much more subtle and level-headed. It is an indirect answer to an uncomfortably direct question.

> Minimalism is the constant art of editing your life.

Minimalism is a reminder that the Cave exists, but it is not an assault on the Cave itself or the people who live in it.

Counter-intuitively, minimalism isn't about minimizing, instead it is about maximizing what really matters in life.

This book offers you a look around and outside of the Cave. Minimalism is a mindset, and this book offers you a toolkit (a series of habits) for making that mindset your own. It is not obvious and it is certainly not easy, but minimalism is available to anyone who is willing to put forth the effort and be brave enough to explore the previously unknown.

Something made you pick up this book. Maybe it was a friend, or maybe it was a deep-seated inclination that there is more to life than just the Cave. You have already taken the first step, now let's dive all the way in.

Chapter 2: It Starts With a Story

As with all important lessons, this one is best expressed by telling a true story.

In 2007 I was battling quite unsuccessfully with clinical depression. I was unhealthy, unhappy, and uninspired. I looked around at the world of adventurers and smiling people displayed online and in the world around me and felt bitterness and resentment. I had barely graduated from high school (a three-time failing of a required math class was conveniently overlooked by an empathetic administrator), and after failing to get out of bed to take a required final college exam, I was on my way to failing out of university. I knew I had a wealth of potential, but I could not figure out how to battle the mental illness that was holding me back.

Depression is a brutal personal illness. Even if you are a strong person it will find your weaknesses. If you are clever, it will find ways to outsmart you. It wins by persistence. Day after day, week after week, depression slowly wears you down. It is relentless and merciless.

At the time, I was young enough to really believe that I could take on and conquer the world all by myself. These strong (and naive) beliefs initially made me resist seeking professional help or medicine. I imagined myself as strong, and I wanted to take the disease on with sheer willpower, not bite-sized pills.

I started by slowly reaching out to people in my life who seemed happy. I had virtually no motivation at the time, so the first people I reached out to were the ones who were already reaching out to me. There was a core group of people in my life who knew something was seriously wrong with me. If they seemed happy, I asked them why. If they were smiling, I asked them where their smile came from.

These turned out to be entirely the wrong questions.

Like depression, happiness is an incredibly personal emotion. It can't be quantified, and as such it is incredibly difficult to explain or reproduce. Asking someone what makes them happy is usually too blunt an exercise and results in generic advice.

By accident, I found a solution to this semantic problem. During one of my talks with a friend, I asked them to tell me one of their favorite life stories. This turned out to be the question I was looking for. Unlike asking someone what makes them happy, asking someone to tell you one of their favorite life stories brings out the light in people's eyes. For the person being asked, it is no longer an intimidating request for sage advice, and more like a request for them to share something they love sharing.

The first story I heard was from my friend, Adam Feldstein. It was a story about his personal quest to attend the top 10 greatest parties in the world. Unlike the often too generic answers to the happiness question, his answer to the favorite life story question was funny, genuine, and easy to relate to. I liked that Adam's answer was different from what I had expected. Adam, who is a self-admitted nerd, does not look like much of a partier. He works at a software company and on a typical work day looks quite unadventurous. He seems to be content with his routine, but at the same time seems mysteriously happy.

Throughout his story he explained that he had actually already attended half of the parties on his list. He described his scanty costumes, his all-night dance marathons, and the absolutely insane people that he had met. He was unable to hold back the biggest smile I had ever seen on him.

After that moment, I was hooked. I took the basis of his story, attend some of the world's greatest parties, and started my own list.[1]

As I continued to ask people to tell me some of their favorite life stories, my list started to grow. See the pyramids in Giza, go sky diving, learn to pickpocket, pilot a plane, live in the wilderness for a month. My list grew and grew.

At some point I reviewed my list and counted the items. I had around 150. They ranged from the simple —get a straight-razor shave—to the very improbable —experience weightlessness.

Inspired by the stories I had heard, I decided to make my list, which I was now calling my Life List; the sole purpose of my life. Whereas a Bucket List is expected to be completed before you die, a morbid goal, a Life List utilizes a deadline which *you* pick to focus on, rather than the uncertain date of your death. I gave myself a deadline, May 25, 2017, got the date tattooed on my butt, and got started.

Since starting that list six years ago, my life has changed dramatically:

Six Years by the Numbers

- 1 Life List item completed every two weeks (on average)
- 10 new people consume my favorite life stories every hour of every day (in the form of videos I produce online, and the writing I do on my blog)
- 100 countries visited
- 1,000 photos taken per trip (on average)
- 10,000 distinct tasks completed per year (see Part Three: Making These Habits Your Habits)
- 100,000 words published on blog (https://www.lifelisted.com/)
- 1,000,000+ miles traveled

I learned how to manage my money and paid off all of my debt (see Chapter 6: Money), lost 60 pounds in a healthy way (see Chapter 21: Food and Chapter 22: Exercise), became an inventor when I filed a patent, ran a marathon, started a company, and experienced weightlessness when I did astronaut training.[2]

You shouldn't believe someone if they tell you they are happy since happiness is expressed through actions and body language, not words, so I am not going to claim to be. That said, my Life List has set me on the path to living a life story that I am genuinely proud of. My Life List gave me a strong enough purpose to eventually beat depression.

A Major Plot Hole

My story of fighting depression is entirely true but also entirely misleading. For those of you who have either dealt with depression or know someone who has, you know that someone cannot simply write a list and will themselves out of mental illness. Even if they could, that will would not help them pay for the items on the list, or magically give them more hours in the day to accomplish their goals.

Real life is not like a Disney movie. Adults have many responsibilities (including but not limited to time and money), many difficulties (time and money) and many limitations (again, time and money).

Like life itself, the journey from depression to happiness is not a straight line. There isn't a formula or clever acronym that magically solves problems. There isn't a seminar you can attend to become immediately successful or a blog post you can read to attain fulfillment. Instead it is a lot of hard work and a lot of trial and error.

Real life journeys look like this:

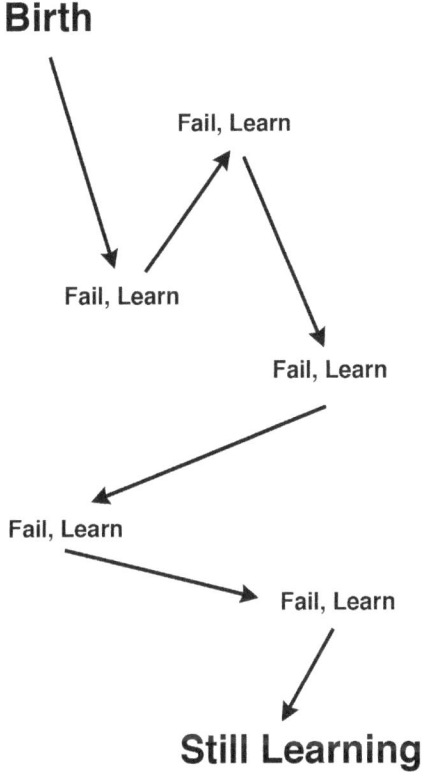

Notice that the end of the chart isn't happiness itself. Happiness isn't a destination. It isn't a place you end up after leveling-up, or a checkbox that you check off after accomplishing even your most well-intentioned dream.

Happiness is the result of a life well lived.

Now we are making progress! A life well lived. That seems like something that is worth attaining. That seems like something that almost anyone would want to aspire to.

After I had written my Life List, but had not yet started completing it, I came to the same conclusion. My new question became how does one live life well?

Chapter 3: How Does One Live Life Well?

The most valuable books from a reading-time to learning ratio are biographies. Autobiographies and biographies are unique; unlike fiction they offer advice from the perspective of actual lives lived. They are based in the real world and the people who are being described had to deal with the same limitations that you and I deal with. (In fact, many of those who lived a life worthwhile enough to warrant a biography had even more limitations than you and I do.)

Reading practically any biography or autobiography will illustrate a uniquely human learning lesson: Life is hard and growth is even harder. This makes real life less like a Hollywood movie and more like a constant stream of good intentions, goofs, and mishaps. This is also why real life doesn't fit into 90 minutes to be enjoyed with popcorn. Real growth takes time, and often times is really ugly.

After struggling unsuccessfully for years, I finally started to make progress on my quest to figure out how to live my life well. The breakthrough happened when I started studying the lives of people who had lived their lives well.

Specifically, I studied their daily routines. I knew that famous people of the past had had the same limitation of 24 hour days that you and I have, and I wanted to figure out how they had accomplished so much given that limitation.

One person that I studied was Benjamin Franklin. Reliable Ben was nice enough to pen an incredibly detailed autobiography that included copious details about his daily routine. As he illustrated in his autobiography, his daily routine was roughly the following:

> *5:00 AM to 8:00 AM: "Rise, wash and address Powerful Goodness[3], contrive day's business, and take resolution of the*

> *day; prosecute the present study, and breakfast.*
>
> *8:00 AM to 12:00 PM: Work.*
>
> *12:00 PM to 2:00 PM: Read, or look over my accounts, and dine.*
>
> *2:00 PM to 6:00 PM: Work.*
>
> *6:00 PM to 10:00 PM: Put things in their places. Supper. Music or diversion, or conversation. Examination of the day.*
>
> *10:00 PM to 5:00 AM: Sleep.*

Was this the secret formula that I had been looking for?

I checked the formula by studying another successful person from the past, Winston Churchill (as preserved by the Churchill Centre[4]):

> *7:30 AM: and remained in bed for a substantial breakfast and reading of mail*

and all the national newspapers. For the next couple of hours, still in bed, he worked, dictating to his secretaries.

At 11:00 AM:, he arose, bathed, and perhaps took a walk around the garden, and took a weak whisky and soda to his study.

At 1:00 PM: he joined guests and family for a three-course lunch. Clementine drank claret, Winston champagne, preferable Pol Roger served at a specific temperature, port brandy and cigars. When lunch ended, about 3:30 PM he returned to his study to work, or supervised work on his estate, or played cards or backgammon with Clementine.

At 5:00 PM:, after another weak whisky and soda, he went to bed for an hour and a half. He said this siesta, a habit gained in Cuba, allowed him to work 1 1/2 days in every 24 hours.

At 6:30 PM: he awoke, bathed again, and dressed for dinner at 8:00 PM

I ran through the exercise of studying the daily routines of famous historical figures again and again.[5]

In the end, I realized something important about the patterns of the daily routines of men and women who had lived life well.

Outside of the fact that all of them slept and ate (almost) every day, there were no important patterns. Again, there was no secret formula. I had again forgotten that I lived in the real world.

I had yet to learn something very important. I was on the right path but I had not yet discovered the mindset that makes up the basis of this book.

Having thought my first quest was a failure, I distracted myself by going on another quest.

Perhaps the key to living life well was by enabling myself with the world's greatest tools. My theory went that having the world's greatest tools would give me the leverage I needed to make efficient use of the limited amount of time I had during the day. I didn't have a lot of money, but I figured that I could invest in the greatest tools in very simple and inexpensive categories.

I couldn't afford the world's greatest car, but I could afford the world's best toothbrush. I couldn't afford the world's best house, but I could afford the world's best belt to keep my pants up. I couldn't afford the world's best computer, but I could provide myself with the world's best pen and paper.

Realizing money was my main limitation to possessing the world's greatest tools, I humored myself by trying to acquire the world's greatest wallet.

I defined what I thought was the criteria for the world's best wallet (thin and indestructible) and reached out to a friend, Craig Chelius, who had already invested a substantial amount of time and money trying to find the perfect wallet.

I met Craig for coffee and explained my quest.

Craig immediately laughed at me.

"I'll save you a lot of time and energy," Craig said, "the most important aspect of a perfect wallet is not what is inside it or included with it, rather the most important aspect is what you subtract from it. You are better off obsessing over what *not* to put into the wallet than you are about what to add to the wallet."

I left our coffee meeting a bit perplexed, but with a slight inkling that I had stumbled onto the gift of a very important idea: addition isn't possible without subtraction.

That night, I thought again about the daily routines that I had been studying earlier. When I did my research, I was only looking at what they had included in their days; I was not seeing what they had intentionally not included in their days. It became so clear, addition isn't possible without subtraction!

Finally, forward progress! I now had a clear direction to move in. It was time to act.

Chapter 4: Addition Isn't Possible Without Subtraction

It was so obvious but had taken me so long to understand. If I wanted to add something to my life, I was going to need to focus on what I would be eliminating first. For example, if I was going to work on one of my Life List items and learn a new foreign language, I was first going to need to figure out what I was going to eliminate from my life.

This turned out to be extremely difficult! In order to fit in language studying, was I going to spend less time with my friends? Sleep less? Watch less TV? I loved my friends and didn't want to see them less. I needed sleep and decreasing it was not something I could reliably or consistently do. TV acted as the downtime I needed to recover from a hard day at work. Skipping it wouldn't allow for the recharge that I needed.

What was I going to eliminate? Something had to go, but it wasn't going to be easy. Everything that was in my current daily routine was there because I needed it there.

This is the ugly section that I left out in the earlier story about my journey out of depression. Like the many books and movies that you have read or seen before, I included the accomplishments of my life but I didn't mention the very important things that I subtracted from my life. Again, in the real world, addition isn't possible without subtraction.

It took me a long time, but eventually I realized that daily life is an endless flow of additions. Co-workers request meetings, advertising fights to sell you more stuff, your friends plan activities for you, your family wants to spend time with you.

All of these things take time and mental energy, they are adding to your already busy schedule.

Benjamin Franklin didn't live life well because he accomplished a lot of things, he lived life well because he subtracted a lot of things and was then able to utilize the freed-up resources to accomplish things that were important and fulfilling.

> "Your net worth to the world is usually determined by what remains after your bad habits are subtracted from your good ones."

- Benjamin Franklin

Like you and I, Benjamin Franklin had a constant barrage of things (including the bad habits of others and himself) trying to add to his already full daily routine. He was successful and lived life well because he actively focused on the subtraction of what was not vital.

I believe that this idea — addition isn't possible without subtraction — is the root cause of all failed good intentions and ambitious goals. To most—the goals they set are worthwhile—but the required subtractions are not. Without the focus on subtraction, the shackles of the Cave keep their hold.

It appeared that the trick to living life well was to focus on what could be subtracted in a world full of needless additions.

This was my first glimpse out of the Cave. This was the first time I experienced the Minimalist Mindset.

Part Two: A Habit Buffet

Chapter 5: All You Can Eat Habits

A mindset is quite different from an idea. Whereas an idea is a mental spark, a mindset is a mental inferno. A mindset is a perspective through which ideas are filtered. An idea can burn out quickly, but a mindset lasts.

The previous portion of this book explained the ignition spark of the Minimalist Mindset, but this book hasn't yet put your hands on the steering wheel.

Just the act of reading a book, no matter how many ideas it contains (or how good looking the author is), is not enough to hold a mindset. To gain a new mindset you need to repeatedly practice habits.

Habits, not ideas, are the programming language of human beings.

The remainder of this book will cover actions and habits for subtracting unnecessary additions from your life. Your willingness to make these habits a part of your life will dictate your ability to access the Minimalist Mindset.

We live in a world that constantly offers additions, thus your focus and efforts are best spent on deciding what to subtract. If you are able to do this well, you will then be able to free up time and money to fill your days with the activities, projects and people that you find meaningful and important. Doing so will enable to you to have a life well lived.

What you choose to prioritize in your life will of course be personal. The pursuit of happiness, after all, is the most personal endeavor anyone can take. There is no one-size-fits-all solution, and there is no magic acronym.

As such, the following chapters are what I call a habit buffet. Like a food buffet, you won't care for everything offered. If you read something that doesn't apply to your priorities, then skip that habit. Not everyone likes tuna noodle casserole. When you run into a habit that you don't like, try simply acknowledging it as an option and then moving forward.

You now have access to a very important idea. Using the habits that follow, it will be up to you to turn that idea into your new mindset. Your chains are now unlocked. It is up to you to summon the courage to walk out of the Cave.

Chapter 6: Money

Every living human being shares the same two overarching limitations, time and money. You can trade time for money (we call this a job) and you can trade money for time (we call this convenience). One of the requirements to living life well is managing these two resources. We will start with the sexier of the two, money.

We begin with one simple economic truth: it is much easier to spend money than it is to earn it. This is the engine that drives the world economy. This is also the best place to start our progress toward getting this limited resource under control.

Conventional money management wisdom recommends eliminating small expenses first. The logic states that if you eliminate your morning $5.00 Starbucks coffee, you will save yourself $1,825.00 a year. ($5.00 multiplied by 365 days equals $1,825.00.) Although this is mathematically true, it fails to acknowledge the full intangible value of the coffee. The purpose of your morning coffee is more than just to provide you with a refreshment. It also helps you establish your cadence for the day. A well structured and productive day is well worth the $5.00 morning ritual.

Instead of eliminating expenses at the bottom, I have found that it is a much more effective habit to eliminate expenses at the top. To do this, you must first identify what are your most expensive but overvalued expenses.

The Single Most Valuable Financial Action

The single most valuable financial action I have ever taken was to create a sorted recurring expenses spreadsheet.

The concept is simple. You are going to identify your recurring expenses and sort them both by the cost and by the true value you received from the expense.

Whichever expense comes out at the top (high cost but low value) of this sort, will be your highest priority expense to eliminate. For the sake of simplicity, we are doing this with only recurring expenses, since over-time they tend to cost you the most money. Also for the sake of simplicity, we are only going to focus on monthly expenses, as annual expenses can be hard to find in bank statements.

If you don't want to create the necessary spreadsheet yourself, you can find a template spreadsheet at https://www.lifelisted.com/min with the name "Recurring Expenses Spreadsheet".

First, get at least two of your monthly bank statements and identify all of the recurring expenses. You can do this by comparing two subsequent statements and identifying the expenses that occur on both.

If, like me, you find expenses on your bank statements that you aren't exactly proud of[6], take the time and effort to forgive yourself.

In the past, you might have been a dummy but that doesn't mean you cannot be forgiven. Human beings make mistakes all of the time. It is part of the human experience. If, when you were a toddler, you made a mistake like tripping and falling down, you probably aren't mad at yourself now. The same logic can be applied when looking at your past bank statements.

Forgive yourself. Let yourself know it was silly and resolve to not make similar mistakes in the future. After that, move forward.

Step 1: Create a spreadsheet of your recurring monthly expenses that includes a column with the name of the expense and a column that contains the monthly cost of the given expense.

Monthly Expense	Cost	Value	True Value
Mortgage/Rent	$750.00		
Online Shopping (Averaged)	$300.00		
Health Insurance	$285.00		
Mobile Phone Service	$120.00		
Monthly Fruit Box	$65.00		
Car (Averaged)	$55.00		
Music Subscription	$9.99		

Next, add a "Value" column and a "True Value" column to the spreadsheet so that you can identify the real value you received from these expenses.

Step 2: Assign each expense a "Value" score between one and three. (Three being expenses that are extremely valuable to your life, one being expenses that are not actually adding real value to your life.)

Monthly Expense	Cost	Value	True Value
Mortgage/Rent	$750.00	3	
Online Shopping (Averaged)	$300.00	1	
Health Insurance	$285.00	3	
Mobile Phone Service	$120.00	2	
Monthly Fruit Box	$65.00	1	
Car (Averaged)	$55.00	1	
Music Subscription	$9.99	1	

Next, use the following equation to populate the fields in the "True Value" column:

$$[(Value/Cost)*100]$$ [7]

Step 3: Finally, sort the spreadsheet by the "True Value" column (ascending) so that the highest cost, lowest value items float to the top. Using our example, the spreadsheet would look like the following:

Monthly Expense	Cost	Value	True Value
Online Shopping (Averaged)	$300.00	1	0.3
Mortgage/Rent	$750.00	3	0.4
Insurance	$285.00	3	1.1
Monthly Fruit Box	$65.00	1	1.5
Mobile Phone Service	$120.00	2	1.7
Car (Averaged)	$55.00	1	1.8
Music Subscription	$9.99	1	10.0

If the spreadsheet is sorted correctly, high "Cost" but low "True Value" items will be at the top. You now have your prioritized list of which expenses to trim. In our example, the two lowest "True Value" expenses were "Online Shopping (Averaged)" and "Mortgage/Rent". These would be the most effective expenses to trim.

> *Note: If this process is too complex, use the template spreadsheet rather than trying to create the spreadsheet yourself. You can find the template spreadsheet at https://www.lifelisted.com/min with the name "Recurring Expenses Spreadsheet."*

I use the word *trim* here intentionally as you will undoubtedly find it is impossible to completely eliminate some expenses. The best example of this is "Mortgage/Rent". You cannot simply ask your landlord or bank to let you stop paying for housing. They will laugh or ignore you. You can't eliminate this expense but you can probably trim it. One way to do this is to switch the payment source of your housing costs to a rewards credit card. *If* you are responsible with credit (this is a very important *if*) and can pay your mortgage or rent with a credit card that gives you one percent back, you have just cut your largest monthly expense by one percent! If you can't pay that expense on a credit card (many mortgage companies disallow this), consider renting out a spare room, moving to a less expensive area, downsizing or any other method that provides you with a better "True Value". See Chapter 9: Housing for an entire chapter dedicated to trimming housing expenses.

This spreadsheet exercise far outweighs the value of cutting out morning coffees and can be used for many areas of your life. See the chapters on food (Chapter 21: Food), transportation (Chapter 10: Transportation) and clothing (Chapter 18: Clothing) for more ideas on trimming your expenses.

Using your prioritized expense spreadsheet you can also more easily make the hard decisions on which expenses can be entirely eliminated.

Doing this exercise once is great, but the goal is to make doing this a habit. (I recommend doing it once every three months.) Life will inevitably throw new expenses your way. It should be your prerogative to focus on identifying which ones are not providing you with enough "True Value", and then acting to trim or entirely eliminate those expenses from your life.

Debt

For many people, interest payments toward debt repayment will be included on their prioritized list of recurring expenses. If debt is on your list, it should be the first expense you fight to defeat.

Debt is a disease. It is stressful, paralyzing, and financially crippling.

The most painful part of debt is that it is a source of stress that is present all of the time, but can only be acted on once or twice a month (dependent on how often you get paid). This makes debt unusually negative.

When I first encountered debt, I downplayed its importance. I made minimum payments and tried my best to ignore it. Unfortunately, this was a losing battle. Even though I tried to ignore it, my debt added an incredible amount of negative financial pressure and stress to my life. Every time I ran myself through the "Recurring Expenses Spreadsheet" exercise, I saw that debt was strangling my freedom. This made it impossible to ignore.

It wasn't until I fully acknowledged that most debt is evil that I started to make strides towards actually conquering it.

Debt is not just an annoying reality, it is the prime example of the shackles that bind people in the Cave.

Debt is the enemy, it is the force sucking your life blood.

Once I realized how horrible debt really was, I started reacting to it like I would react to a swarm of bees attacking my face. It instantly became my top priority and my sole focus.

I made some bold changes in my financial lifestyle, put myself on voluntary house arrest, temporarily gave up all of my hobbies, became obsessed with cutting costs, and was forced to spend less time with my friends and girlfriend. Subtraction of my debt became my main temporary focus.

After four months of reacting to the metaphorical killer bee attack, I was able to pay off all of my remaining debt.

It was an insane reaction but it was what was necessary to free myself.

If you have debt, take a moment and consider how much negativity and stress it is bringing to your life. When you see your debt balance do you quietly feel shame, and distract yourself with something else (like I originally did), or do you acknowledge a real danger to your freedom and fight back?

If you are ready to fight for your freedom, fight like the bees are already here.

Eliminate Expenses at Their Source

After you are done trimming and eliminating expenses (debt being the most important), your next highest value financial action is to simplify your spending abilities.

The more ways you have to spend, the more you are likely to spend. Before I started to eliminate my spending abilities I had three credit cards, two debit cards, countless gift cards, about $100.00 worth of coins, and about $500.00 in various currencies that I kept telling myself I would convert back into my normal currency one day. All of this was of course a huge financial blunder.

I had so many ways to spend money that I would frequently lose track of my expenses. Even worse, my accounts were so diluted that I was unable to make large purchases on any of them without incurring debt. Even when I received paychecks I would frequently run into cash flow issues.

I had recurring expenses for services I didn't even know I had, and currencies (both literal and in the form of gift cards) that were effectively valueless to me.

It was a big mess.

To remedy this, I blocked off three evenings on my calendar and vowed to get my personal financial system under control.

During the first two evenings, I eliminated all but

one debit card, one credit card, two checking accounts, and two investment accounts I then went to my local bank and deposited all of my coins. The bank tellers made me sort and wrap the coins, but that wasn't a big deal.

During the same bank visit, I exchanged all of my foreign currencies. I previously thought you could only do this at the airport where they charge outrageous fees. It turns out you can do this at most major banks for much more reasonable fees.

I sold all of my gift cards online[8] and closed all of my bank accounts except for two checking accounts (one master account, explained shortly, and one extra expenses account) and two investment accounts (one that is low risk to be used as a safety net and one that is higher risk that is used to for retirement funds).

At the time of writing this book, most savings accounts offered in the United States are worse than useless. (The same is true of most other developed countries as well.) The interest rate that they earn is typically less than the applicable rate of inflation which means you are actually losing money every year that your cash sits in those accounts.

Don't ignore that last idea. A "savings" account which offers less than a 1% interest rate loses you money when you realize inflation in many countries is usually more than 1%. For context, at the time of writing, the best savings account publicly available by my major bank in the United States is 0.06%[9], and the current inflation rate in the United States is 1.5%[10]. This is comparable to robbery!

This mismatch is a mean but profitable trick that the banks are playing on the public. The bank makes money from your savings account but you probably don't.

As an alternative to a traditional savings account, I found it to be a better option to use two investment accounts. The first account is low risk and I use it as a safety net and large planned expense fund. The second investment account is higher risk (which theoretically means higher returns) and is for retirement funds. Both accounts are made up of low-cost index funds from Vanguard, a great option for my particular circumstance. That said, please consult with a well regarded fiduciary in your area to determine where to invest your funds.

It did take three evenings to get my personal finance system simplified but the resulting system (one debit card, one credit card, two checking accounts, and two investment accounts) meant that I had better visibility and thus better control over my expenses. I credit this systematic change to saving me just about as much money as the expenses that I directly cut using the prioritized spreadsheet exercise.

Automate Good Habits

After you have a clear sense of which of your expenses are actually valuable, as well as having your financial system under control, you can start to automate your good financial habits.

Automating good habits refers to having technology automatically do the work you know you should be doing but probably won't. The prime examples of this in personal finance are with savings, investing, and credit card payments. Instead of leaving it on yourself to remember to save or invest money, have your bank do it for you automatically as an automated transfer. For the majority of big banks, automated transfers are a free service that only require setting up once. Thus, setting up a system that fits your needs can automate good financial habits for the rest of your life.

For me, the order of operations looks like this:

29th Day Of The Month (Direct Deposit): My paycheck is direct deposited into my master checking account. This deposit acts as the fuel for my personal finance system.

1st Day Of The Month (Automatic Transfer): My bank transfers $1,000.00 from my master checking account to my secondary checking account where I can draw on it to pay for normal life non-recurring expenses. By intentionally limiting my spending access to this secondary account rather than my master checking account, I decrease my ability to overspent. Notice that I am intentionally paying myself first. I do this so that my level of financial stress remains low and I have the ability to make necessary purchases to keep my projects moving forward.

4th Day Of The Month (Automatic Transfer): My bank transfers the maximum legal amount to my retirement investment account. This is an example of automating my good habits. This transfer happens automatically and is essentially invisible to me.

4th Day Of The Month (Automatic Transfer): My bank transfers $500.00 to my secondary investment account (which is also my safety net and large planned expense fund). This automatic transfer is also an example of automating my good habits as saving for a better future happens without me having to do any additional work.

5th Day Of The Month (Automatic Payment): My bank automatically transfers money to pay off my credit card in full. Most big banks offer this feature for free but you need to opt-in to it. I have *all* of my recurring expenses go through my credit card so that I can keep them in a centralized place and so that I can get reward points from these necessary expenses. The payment of my credit card intentionally happens after I have received my paycheck and after I have transferred money into my investing account. As long as I don't overspend on my credit card, this step prevents me from ever having to worry about needing to pay credit card interest on debt.

Every month these transfers happen without me having to do anything. My paycheck is automatically deposited into my master checking account and the money automatically trickles into other accounts that automatically perform good actions for me. This happens regardless of where I am located on the planet, and regardless of whether or not I have an Internet connection or phone service. Now that I have this system in place, it actually would require more work to stop the system that is performing my good habits than it would to just let it run in the background without my intervention. In this way, my money manages itself so that I can use my time on things that are actually important.

Periodically I review this system to make sure my setup is still aligned with my current priorities. When I do these reviews, I transfer any excess money that has accumulated in my master checking account to my safety net investment account so that I can be prepared for whatever the future brings.

Remember, when you spend money, you are really trading the hours you worked to earn that money for whatever it is you are buying. The available hours of your life are always decreasing so make sure your trades are actually worth the exchange.

Chapter 7: Time

Every year, Tony Robbins (author, movie star, and seminar leader) hosts an elite mastermind of some of the world's most successful people at his private island in Fiji. He invites adventurers, world leaders, and billionaires to come to his island and exchange resources and ideas. Although each group can benefit equally from the gathering—every year the latter group—the billionaires—have the fewest showings. While they have effectively solved the problem of money in their lives, they have become slaves to their schedules. They have traded one type of shackle for another.

To a lesser degree this same problem happens in most people's lives. As we grow up and take on more time responsibilities in exchange for money, we lose the time resources that seemed abundant when we were young.

The source of this "time leak" is time commitments. Be it a full time job or just a hobby, responsibilities soak up our precious waking hours. Individually these decisions make sense. If you love a specific hobby—say tutoring aspiring pinball players—then it does not seem like much of a sacrifice to devote each of your Tuesday evenings to this pursuit. In isolation, this may be a great use of time.

Like many problems, this one only surfaces in the aggregate. A planned activity once a week is not a problem, but seven different activities, each taking place on a different night, become a big time problem. Saying no to any of the activities individually is rough, and saying no in aggregate can feel virtually impossible.

It is for this reason that you need to be ruthless about managing your time commitments. You have goals, family responsibilities, and spiritual journeys that you want to enjoy in your life. Remember that addition is not possible without subtraction. The only way to prioritize the important pursuits is to say no to the less important ones.

Unfortunately, saying no is hard, very hard.

The single best solution I have for this difficult problem is having a well thought-out auto response. This solves the problem and is easier on your conscience than having to think up a new excuse each time someone asks for your time. You can use my script as an example for your own:

> *This is uncomfortable but I am actually booked solid with previous commitments at the moment. :-/ I don't like having a schedule like this so I am actively fighting it by not taking on any new commitments right now.*
>
> *That said, feel free to reach out to me again in a month and we can meet up after my schedule calms down.*
>
> *Thanks for your understanding! (This isn't anything personal! Promise!)*
>
> *Best Regards,*
>
> *- Danny*

Depending on the circumstance, you can either speak this script or send it via e-mail. To make this even easier on yourself, create a shortcut in your e-mail program in order to make this happen with only a few keystrokes.

See https://www.lifelisted.com/min and look for the tools listed under "Text Expanders" for instructions on how to do this in many common operating systems.

One Step Blocker

While the aforementioned technique works well for many engagements, it isn't very effective at combating short term commitments like co-workers asking for meetings. You can't just simply say no to every meeting your co-workers ask you to attend. For these instances I have another technique that I call the One Step Blocker.

When a co-worker or stranger invites me to a meeting that I don't think will be particularly valuable, I respond with a polite request asking them to provide a meeting agenda before I accept the invitation. This simple and reasonable request is almost universally effective.

The vast majority of requesters are too lazy to take the extra step, and end up never re-inviting me to the meeting that would likely have been a waste of my time anyway. For those who do send an agenda, I attend the meeting and everyone involved is better off because there is now an established and thought out agenda for what will be covered. This technique is a rare real life win-win situation for everyone involved.

This habit alone is responsible for freeing up more of my previously wasted work-related time than any other time related habit in this book. It is one of the most powerful habits I know to build and maintain the Minimalist Mindset.

Beware of the Spotted Cat Schedule

Meetings are not inherently a bad thing. Communication is critical to any pursuit, and meetings are a useful way of exchanging information. That said, they do have downsides. Each meeting, even when it includes an agenda, requires some amount of transition both before and after it takes place. This involves both logistical transitions (getting to the right place) as well as mental transitions (loading up the right information into one's head). This is frequently called the cost of context switching[11].

The biggest problem with many people's schedules is that they are splattered with random meetings. Their calendars look like the fur patterns of spotted cats. A meeting may only be scheduled to take 30 minutes but many times they require an additional 30 minutes of context transitions. This is absolutely crippling to creative productivity and mental clarity. If one's day is spotted with random meetings, it may become impossible to gather the mental resources to pursue activities that require real creative thought.

I have encountered this problem as both a developer (I am a Rubyist) and as a writer. Many days I was unable to do my job simply because I was stuck spending nearly my entire day transitioning from one low-to-moderately important task to another.

To solve this context switching problem, I now implement a strict meetings-only day each week. With rare exceptions, I only accept meetings (both in-person and phone calls) on Wednesdays. I realize that some meetings are important so I can't eliminate them entirely; however, I can schedule them for a single day each week to eliminate many of the interruptions in my creative process.

If I run out of meeting spots on a given Wednesday (which happens far too often), I start scheduling meetings for the following Wednesday. The upside to this time management strategy is that it gives me six full days to concentrate on my creative work pursuits every week. As a result, my creative productivity has skyrocketed. The downside to this is that I know I will not have creative times on Wednesdays and thus don't look forward to the middle of the week.

If your work culture or responsibilities make it unfeasible to get meetings down to a single day during the week, do your best to condense them into as few days as possible. Even one meeting-free day can be a great gift to your creative productivity. To do this, schedule full day "blocked" events on your own shared calendar so that your co-workers cannot schedule meetings with you on the given days. This works especially well at big companies where people assume that any free time on someone else's calendar is fair game to schedule a meeting.

Unlike money, time is a resource that slowly but constantly decreases. For many people, this makes it the most valuable resource of all. For that reason, it is incredibly important to prioritize it before it runs out. No one looks back at the end of their life and is happy about how many hours they spent in meetings. Start prioritizing the habit of time management now. Otherwise, you may never have the opportunity.

Chapter 8: Work

Minimizing employment responsibilities is the hardest step to becoming a successful holistic minimalist. In many cultures (specifically: American, Japanese, and Singaporean), the amount of hours one works is seen as a benchmark for measuring success. This runs counter to the goals of minimalism.

From a minimalist point of view, employment should serve only two goals:

- Funding that which allows you to live life well
- Attaining fulfillment

Any work that doesn't lead to you accomplishing your most important goals is wasted energy and accumulates unnecessary stress.

While the theory of this might seem simple, making it a reality is not. Bosses don't tend to care about employee happiness unless it is related to employee retention. Furthermore, for almost all businesses a primary objective is to maximize revenue generated per employee. This makes sense for the business, but doesn't serve the goals of the would-be minimalist on the other end of the equation.

So how does one escape these very real shackles?

Building a Minimalist Business

The financial goal of a business is to leverage assets to create profit. Opposingly, the financial goal of an individual is to leverage assets (mainly time and skills) to trade for goods and services that may increase happiness.

This difference is seemingly small but incredibly important. People are generally good at spending money, whereas businesses are generally good at making money. After all, the goal of much of personal finance (extracting happiness through the consumption of goods and services) runs counter to the goal of business finance (maximize profits). As such, business structures are a better tool for maximizing wealth than the normal personal processes (i.e., working for someone else).

Remember, you can either work to achieve your own dreams, or you can work for someone else and help them achieve their dreams.

Generally, entrepreneurship is framed as a competition to create the biggest and most profitable business possible. This is a popular path but it is not the only way. The other direction (and the better minimalist direction) is to aim to create a tiny business that is aimed only to provide the minimal profits necessary to facilitate your well lived life. Minimalist businesses don't require big budgets or many employees. Instead, they are intentionally structured to remain small so that they don't require unwanted responsibilities or stresses. A minimalist business doesn't inherently strive to make you a millionaire, but it does strive to maximize your time, freedom, and provide you with enough money to cover your needs.

Identify how much money you personally need to reach the two minimalist goals of employment (funding that which allows you to live life well and attaining personal fulfillment). Then, seek to build a minimalist business that covers that and only that. Identify what value you can provide to the world and charge others for it. You don't need a large team, you only need yourself and some people who are willing to pay for the value you provide them.

While this is the ideal solution, it is important to

note that entrepreneurship is not the right path for everyone. Being your own boss is both a blessing and curse. It inherently requires more upfront effort than being an employee, and it comes with a lot of uncertainty and very little stability. If this doesn't fit with your life context, your next best option is to be a highly leveraged employee.

Becoming a Highly Leveraged Employee

It is unrealistic to expect that everyone can be their own boss. The world's businesses need employees in order to flourish. More importantly, certain lifestyles require an amount of stability that is not possible with entrepreneurship. The solution to this is to be a highly leveraged employee.

Do you want a higher salary? Do you want to work remotely? Do you want to not have to work on Fridays? If you do, you need to become so valuable to your company that they can't say no to your requests. You need to gain so much leverage that there is no feasible way for them to deny your reasonable requests. There are at least three ways to do this:

1. Own a key project or system
2. Have an incredibly high work output
3. Be the best problem solver at the company

The fastest way to build high leverage is to own a key company project or system. If a key business objective cannot be completed without you, then you have leverage to ask for better working terms. Common examples of this are building human relationships the company needs to succeed (typically done by salespeople and governmental policy makers), managing a key business technology system (typically done by programmers and database engineers), or running a long term and complex business program (typically done by accountants and human resource professionals). Your goal is to either find one of these openings at your current company, or find another company that has one of these opportunities available. The key to finding these opportunities is to be willing to step outside of your expected job requirements and to take on high value responsibilities that no one else at the company is willing or able to do.

The next best way to build high leverage is to have an incredibly high work output. Can you output twice as much high quality work than your co-workers? For many professions, this is much easier than it sounds. People tend to output just as much as they are expected to output. Many people wait until just before deadlines to do work. Many people refuse to step outside of their established job description. You do not need to be one of those people. Minimalism is largely about establishing your real priorities and cutting away everything that does not serve those goals. If you can prove to your boss that you are more valuable than your co-workers, you can reasonably ask for more freedom and flexibility with your job. If they say no, there is likely a competitor out there that would love to hire the high-outputting you.

The last way to build leverage as an employee is more abstract than the others. Every business has problems and all business owners want those problems solved. Therefore, you can build your leverage by becoming the best problem solver at the company. This applies to all industries. This strategy requires a lot more upfront work and a certain degree of bravado. You will need to step out of your comfort zone and step on the toes of others who are causing or facilitating problems. There is no formula for achieving this; it is a mindset. What problems can you solve at your company? This should be a never-ending question.

To get started on this, challenge yourself to provide your manager with two solutions to problems for every one problem you bring them. They will be grateful and you will start building your leverage.

Workplace Popcorn

> *Note: This habit really only applies to knowledge workers who have flexibility with their workplaces. If this doesn't apply to you, skip this habit and go to the next one in the habit buffet.*

Even on my most productive days, I always hit a mental wall several hours after I start working. When I hit this mental wall, my work stumbles to a stop and I struggle to maintain focus on the given action. The duration between mental walls vary by people and situation, but they do present themselves eventually. Luckily, there is a simple strategy for overcoming them.

Most of the time, mental walls are less mental than they are physical. Simply standing up, taking a walk, or going to a new location (even if it is in the same building) are generally all that is necessary to overcome common mental walls. Blogger and adventurer Joel Runyon[12] came up with this idea and named it Workplace Popcorn. The concept is that when you get to your wall, you react like a popcorn kernel and "pop" over to a new location. Now whenever I hit my daily mental wall, I get up and go to a new room or even a new cafe to continue my work. This strategy has proven invaluable both for my productivity and my physical health.

Minimalist Workspace

Your workspace can have as much impact on your ability to do your work as the work that needs to get done. For a minimalist workspace, I focus on two goals:

- Eliminate barriers to doing work
- Eliminate distractions

These goals are more examples of focusing on subtraction rather than addition. While many people focus on something like adding a walking desk to their office to increase productivity, the wiser minimalist focuses on subtraction by identifying what they can eliminate from their workspace.

Be a Stickler about Eliminating Work Barriers

When it comes to business productivity, there are few experiences that are worse than finally getting yourself into your workflow (which sometimes can take all day) and then realizing that you are missing a critical tool required for your work. Depending on the nature of your work this can be a physical tool, or it can be intangible, like a required password. Common solutions to this problem include:

- Having immediate access to duplicates of your

critical physical tools in case they break
- Storing all of your files, passwords (encrypted), and software in the cloud for access anywhere

While this won't be possible for all jobs, it should be a general principle that you apply as widely as possible. Remember, getting into a flow is a hard enough objective! As such, you should go far out of your way to avoid the potential for this situation to occur.

Be a Stickler about Eliminating Distractions

Distractions are the perfect poison. They can take the form of practically anything, and they can ruin the best of intentions. Therefore, when you are trying to work you need to actively fight to avoid and eliminate distractions. This means avoiding both physical distractions (most notably distracting people) and intangible distractions (noises, visual cues and other notifications). The methods for doing this will vary by the nature of the work being done, but key areas to focus on are:

- Co-workers (see Chapter 23: Friends)
- Working environment (See the rest of this chapter)
- Mobile phones (see Chapter 13: Mobile Phone)

- Your schedule (see Chapter 7: Time)

When you encounter distractions from these sources, you need to prioritize eliminating their effects on your ability to work. Just accepting or temporarily ignoring them is not enough. Distracting you once is annoying, but distracting you repeatedly is detrimental to your work. The small distractions add up and can have a large negative impact on your well-being and ability to complete work.

The second part of this is more abstract. In addition to eliminating distractions, I also actively train myself to separate the tools I use for working and the tools I use for playing. Depending on the nature of the work to be done, the implementation for this will vary. For some, this is being diligent about only doing work while in a physical office. They reserve play for other physical spaces or other rooms within the same building. Other people pick one cafe for working and then designate all other cafes for casual play and get-togethers. Others will use one Internet browser for work and a different browser for reading articles and social media. Still others mix spaces but designate certain tools for work and others for play. This can be separate computers if your budget affords it, or can be something free like having a work music playlist. The goal here is to train your body and mind to associate certain objects, tools, spaces, or feelings with work so that you can get into your flow as fast as possible.

Chapter 9: Housing

For many people, moving day is one of the most stressful but exciting days of their lives. Moving is a tangible expression of internal change. Often this is a positive change where we upgrade our lifestyles and enter a new chapter in our lives. As measured by the American Dream, an upgrade in lifestyle is an upgrade in life. Unfortunately, this measurement doesn't tell the whole story.

A step upwards in housing is not always a step upwards in life. Bigger homes require more expensive insurance, more furniture, and more time spent maintaining them. The journey from living with your parents, to getting your first apartment, to getting your first home is like an escalator. It feels like forward progress, but is really a one-way trip. Like riding an escalator upwards, moving up in lifestyle feels easy, but trying to fight the trend and moving down in lifestyle is incredibly hard.

This upward momentum typically leads to a life with an abundance of objects and bills, but a deficit of freedom and fulfillment. It is all too often a path that leads to the situation in the Cave. This chapter will explain how to get off of this path.

Using Travel as a Forcing Function

So how does one protect themselves from this societal trap? The best strategy I know for keeping your lifestyle in check is to prioritize travel.

Travel has many benefits. The most important of these are exposing yourself to other cultures, opening your mind to new ideas, learning that life offers many ways of living, and giving you the opportunity to learn about yourself by seeing yourself through other people's eyes.

Travel also acts as a forcing function. If you are going to leave your home for several weeks, you are forced to objectively evaluate your lifestyle. If you have too many home maintenance responsibilities (pets, plants, objects) you will quickly learn what is detracting from your freedom. Preparing for travel shines a useful but uncomfortable spotlight on how far up the escalator of lifestyle you have traveled.

Like all big life changes, the best way to get started traveling is to start small. Start by being a tourist in your own town. See the sights, explore new neighborhoods, and try a few new places to eat. Once you gain more momentum, travel to a nearby town or city. Be a stranger and look at your environment with new eyes. After you have done that, go as far as your resources allow.

Start the habit of travel now so that you intentionally feel the burden of the lifestyle escalator. When you feel that burden, it makes it much easier to prioritize a fix. Making this a habit allows you to identify small burdens that are easily subtracted.

Traveling also lets you check the validity of your living condition assumptions. Do you perhaps assume that it would be infeasible to live in a smaller house? Try renting a smaller place in a less expensive foreign country for a week and see if you are able to deal with the smaller space. If that isn't currently possible, stay a weekend at a friend's house and compare the differences between your own home and your friend's home. What does your friend not have that you can go without? Chances are there will be more than you think. Are you thinking that it is impossible to live without an expensive appliance, like a clothes dryer? Try going a week without one (air drying), or if possible, visit a country that doesn't use them.

If traveling is not an option for you, consider

implementing one of the the following habits to get similar housing effects:

- Remove one light bulb in a room that is already well lit.
- Program or add a piece of tape to your thermostat so that it has a lower maximum heat setting. You can do the same to set a minimum cooling setting for your air conditioning.
- Experiment with avoiding the entering of a specific room for a set period of time.
- Clean out one drawer or closet and resolve not to use it.
- Designate your garage as only a place for your car.

Exposing yourself to alternative housing concepts allows you to check the validity of any assumptions you may be making about what is actually necessary to live well.

Chapter 10: Transportation

Like the pressures of housing, many societies constantly push people to upgrade their modes of transportation. Expensive cars are viewed as a sign of success and stability. This is fine in and of itself, but when coupled with the fact that many societies ceaselessly push people to upgrade, we run into the same problem as before; it is easy to go up but extremely difficult to go down on the lifestyle escalator.

Optimal transportation options are entirely dependent on circumstance. For some people, cycling to work is a great option, for others using public transportation or driving a big car are the best options. As long as you can get from point A to point

B reliably and within a personally acceptable set of criteria (time, cost, convenience), then you have succeeded at maximizing your approach to transportation.

The Battle over Your Commute

According to the 2014 American Community Survey[13], an ongoing statistical survey by the U.S. Census Bureau, Americans spent an average of 26 minutes commuting to work every day. When looked at over the time-span of a year, the average travel time to and from work for American commuters in 2014 was 13,520 minutes (or just under 9.4 entire days). This is 28.14 work days (9.4 full days / 8-hour work days) that workers commuted without either getting paid for their time or being reimbursed for their expenses.

Over 10 years, this adds up to 94 days spent only driving to and from work! Your numbers may vary but if you commute it is important to realize how those minutes add up and that the corresponding time could otherwise be spent with your friends or family.

This huge sacrifice does not account for the money spent on gasoline, vehicle maintenance, and insurance (one report[14] pegs this number at $125,000, although it uses a longer than average commute), and it also does not account for the time spent away from loved ones (one Swedish dissertation from Umea University[15], which sampled two million households in Sweden, concluded that the risk of divorce is 40 percent higher among long-distance commuters than among other couples).

The numbers are disheartening, but you don't need them to realize that commuting is a big sacrifice. Commuting is stressful and aggravating.

As such, consider some of the other options that may exist for your personal work context:

- Living closer to where you work
- Cycling to work (so you can get exercise while commuting)
- Taking public transport (so you can work or study while commuting)
- Working from home
- Getting a new job that has a shorter commute
- Using a combination of these techniques on various days

The real battle over personal transportation comes in the form of figuring out the best way for you to transport yourself while balancing personal freedom and personal convenience. You will constantly feel pressure to upgrade or change your modes of transportation. Your battle will be actively working to remain content with what you have. Ultimately, it is not the size of your wheels that matter, it is how you are using them and where you are going with them that will make an important impact on your life.

Chapter 11: Communication

Clear and consistent communication is absolutely essential for every kind of human relationship. As such, improving your communication habits are a disproportionately valuable personal investment.

Establish Your Response Times

The biggest cause for communication overload is a failure to set expectations about how any given communication channel will be treated. I use the following rules for my main communication channels. (Yours might vary but feel free to use mine as a starting point.) I rarely directly state these rules to people—instead I set expectations by consistent response times. For example, I teach, over time, that calling me will yield a much faster response than e-mailing me.

My Communication Response Time Rules:

Medium	Response Time
Phone Calls	1 Hour
Text Messages	2 Hours
Instant Messages	2 Hours
E-mail Messages	1 Day
Social Media Interactions	1 Day
Postal Mail	2 Weeks

These may seem slow to you. This is intentional. Communication is a neutral productive task. It is useful, but it is rarely important work by itself.

My response times are intentionally inversely related to how many people have access to me via a given channel. For example, while my response time with phone calls is relatively fast, the number of people who have my phone number is relatively low. I keep my phone number as private as possible by not including it in my e-mail signature and not listing it online. Additionally, I opt-in to national Do Not Call lists, and if I receive a phone call from an unknown number I force it to voicemail. I do all of this in order to keep my volume of calls low so that I can maintain a fast response time.

Conversely, my response time with postal mail is slow but the amount of people that have access to my postal address (my public business address) is high. This relationship is a function of scaling. I can only maintain these response times if the amount of incoming communications stays proportionally the same between the access of channels.

By reducing the amount of time you spend communicating (a neutrally productive task), you increase the amount of time you have available for doing more creative and forward moving work (positive productive tasks).

At this point we are still outlining the bigger picture best practices for communication, but don't worry, we go into specific best practices for two of the hardest channels in the chapters on e-mail (Chapter 12: E-mail) and mobile phones (Chapter 13: Mobile Phone). But before we get to those, let's focus on how you can make all of your communication better.

Simple Methods for Communicating Better

There are two simple things that most people can do to become better communicators:

1. Listen to others more
2. Ask better questions

The order of these is important. You generally can't ask better questions unless you have already taken the time to listen well.

How to Become a Better Listener

Listening is like all other skills; it can be improved through practice. The key to getting better at listening is to put effort into not just hearing the words that someone is speaking, but trying to understand the holistic perspective of where those words are coming from. Understanding and empathy are the signs of good listening, not just the ability to repeat the words that have been spoken.

If you want to improve your listening, actively challenge yourself to empathize more and talk less during conversations. Hear the words others are saying and rather than applying their meaning to your world, take the extra initiative and try to feel the world of the other person who spoke the given words. It is not initially easy, but it does get easier with practice.

How to Ask Better Questions

After you have improved your listening skills, you can then start improving the questions you ask. There is one key element that separates a good question from a bad question. A good question should both elicit understanding in the question being asked and cause new understanding once it is answered. Good questions convey important information in both directions.

Bad questions do just the opposite—they are generic and are usually asked and answered without much conscious effort or transference of valuable information by either person participating.

For example, rather than asking someone how their day was (a bad question because the question does not elicit understanding or promote new understanding in the answer), it would be better to start with some context and then ask how they specifically were impacted by the example. This might sound like: Wow, that workload was much harder than usual today. Given how difficult your job is normally, what kept you pushing to make it through today?

In order to get better at asking questions, focus your efforts on listening. After you have a better understanding of another person's perspective, you can then start asking them questions that will warrant deeper thought and more valuable responses. The following are some simple methods for asking valuable questions:

- Ask "why" rather than "how"
- Ask about feelings rather than facts
- Ask for additional details of information that has already been conveyed

While you can get better at communicating, it is not a skill that you can flat-out perfect. That is part of the beauty of this very real skill. Communication is vital to every type of relationship (business, romantic, social, etc.) and as such, improvements you make to your communication skills will help you in many areas of your life.

Now that we have discussed some of the high level best practices for communication, let's get into how this can apply to more specific areas of your life.

Chapter 12: E-mail

E-mail is the single biggest culturally accepted time-waster of this century. This technology allows any one of the billions of people with Internet access (and countless automated scripts) to add something to your to-do list. Even by just erasing an e-mail in your inbox, you waste mental energy both deciding to delete it and in transitioning to the next decision.

It might sound like heresy in many industries, but e-mail should not be your most important priority. It is a task that never ends. It is an electronic leash that takes away from the free time you have earned to be with your friends and family. The e-mail that seems so important today will undoubtedly be trumped by another e-mail tomorrow.

One and Done

The best action you can take to minimize the adverse effects of e-mail in your life is to never, ever, read an individual e-mail more than once. Instead, read it once and then instantly act on it by doing one of the following:

- Mark it as spam - This decreases the chances you will get similar e-mails in the future. In many cases, in addition to marking it as spam you should also unsubscribe from the applicable newsletter or list. If an e-mail wastes your time once, take the extra step of unsubscribing or marking it as spam so that it never has the opportunity to waste your time again.
- Archive it - Do this if no specific question was asked of you in the e-mail.
- Convert it into an action item - Plan on doing this task only after you have finished processing your inbox.
- Delegate it to someone else - Is the ask in the e-mail something you absolutely need to do yourself? Is there anyone else who can do this work for you?
- Reply to it - This should be a last resort, as replies tend to lead to more replies which means more e-mail.

No exceptions, break the "re-read" habit and get that e-mail out of your life altogether!

See https://www.lifelisted.com/min under the heading "E-mail Tools" for the latest and greatest e-mail tools.

Protect Your E-mail Address like Cell Phone Users Protect Their Phone Numbers

Gone are the days when everyone's private telephone number was publicly listed. While landlines are still listed in the yellow pages for telemarketers to harvest, mobile phone numbers are more heavily guarded. This became necessary after telemarketing was abused and people became angry.

Oddly, today's e-mail addresses have been abused too, but for some reason people still feel like they should post their e-mail addresses on all of their communications for the whole world to harvest. You have other options.

Make Yourself Hard to E-mail

The best action you can take to save yourself from e-mail is to make yourself hard to e-mail. With the exception of a business e-mail address, it is not advantageous to advertise your e-mail address on social media and your website. If someone wants to contact you, either have them fill out a simple web form or make them dig a little bit on your website to find your e-mail address. This might sound snobby, but it will save you countless hours that would potentially be wasted due to the horrendous noise-to-signal ratio of most people's e-mail inboxes.

Have Software Prioritize Your Inbox

With regard to your inbox itself, I highly recommend using a set of prioritized inboxes.

Instead of manually prioritizing your inbox every day, have software determine what is important for you. This might sound like the beginning of a scary artificial intelligence sci-fi scene, but you will likely be surprised by how effective (nor deadly) e-mail prioritization algorithms are. Software has the ability to create one primary inbox for you which you can act on daily, and one secondary inbox which you can act on every other day. Nothing gets deleted or pushed into a hidden spam folder, but every e-mail gets prioritized. I was highly skeptical at first, but have since been convinced and fully trust this type of software. Using this technology I can spend more time acting on what is necessary and less time filtering.

Since the best software for achieving this changes much faster than I can update this book, see https://

www.lifelisted.com/min under the heading "E-mail Tools" for the latest and most useful e-mail tools for prioritizing your inbox.

Relentlessly Unsubscribe

It is bad enough to have an unwanted newsletter waste your time once, it is far worse to have it waste your time repeatedly. Be relentless about protecting your inbox by unsubscribing as often as possible. The simple act of clicking unsubscribe in an e-mail footer can save you countless wasted impressions of an extraneous newsletter or thread in the future.

Better yet, have software do this for you. I am a bit crazy about optimizing my e-mail so I jump on new tools as soon as they come out. See https://www.lifelisted.com/min under the heading "E-mail tools" for the most useful e-mail auto-unsubscribe tools.

Minimize Your E-mail Surface Area

One of the biggest causes of e-mail overload is having too many e-mail addresses. This increases your e-mail surface area and makes you dangerously easy to e-mail. Many people have work e-mail addresses, personal e-mail addresses, and many times a host of other legacy e-mail accounts. This is a problem that slowly creeps forward and gets worse. The best action you can use to protect yourself (mainly your time) is to either redirect your extraneous inboxes to one central inbox, or to delete your extraneous accounts altogether. Modern email providers are even smart enough to check which e-mail address an incoming e-mail was sent to and automatically send your reply message from that e-mail address. This way your work and personal e-mail accounts stay segregated while maintaining one e-mail inbox.

Now that we have covered tips for minimizing your e-mail, let's attack another scary time-wasting beast, mobile phones.

Chapter 13: Mobile Phone

    Cell phones are, at present, our greatest modern tool for distraction and time-waste. They literally take all of our communication channels and put them in our pockets. With the best of the virtual world in your pocket, this creates an unending desire to check in on what is happening. If you are having a lackluster moment in real life, why not just look at your phone and find something better? While this is not inherently bad, the distraction situation does become problematic when it distracts us from meaningful or productive work. Small breaks are healthy, but incessant distractions can prevent us from actually living.

Silence Distractions

The single best thing you can do to eliminate the distractions caused by cell phones is to disable notifications from e-mail, games, social media, and anything else that alerts you from your phone. This includes both the audio notifications and the visual badge notifications. This doesn't mean you won't receive new communications, it just means that you won't be interrupted when they arrive. If it's appropriate in your life context, consider completely removing social media applications from your mobile device. This will force social media activities to become an intentional activity rather than a boredom induced reaction.

A Nightly Peace Setting

The next best thing you can do to eliminate the distractions caused by your cell phone is to schedule a Do Not Disturb time. This is a built-in feature that is freely available on both iOS and Android based phones. (You can find step-by-step instructions at https://www.lifelisted.com/min) You simply set a timespan, say 1:00 AM to 7:00 AM, and your phone's audio will be muted during that time frame. As a safety precaution, it is useful to set exceptions for important contacts and for unknown numbers that call you multiple times in a row (both of these are also built in and free features of modern phone operating systems).

Become a Social Media Snob

If you are an extremist like me, you can go as far as to not have social media apps on your phone. (Remember, if absolutely necessary you can always access the web version of social media websites.) While socially strange in some circles, this will free you up to experience the real world as you are living it. You can always take photos and videos on your phone and share them later; there is rarely a need to do it in real-time. Remember, urgent and important are different attributes.

Audit Your Apps

While a multitude of new apps are added daily to the various app marketplaces, your phone's screen real estate and hard drive constraints remain constant. It is a battle and we are all on the losing end.

To combat the influx of new apps, I have found it important to make it a habit to conduct a quick monthly app audit. I force myself to delete at least one app a month. This keeps efficiency and effectiveness on my phone high, and new distractions to a minimum. It also has the added benefit of keeping my battery life high, as fewer apps running means less energy consumed.

The app auditing process will vary by person so I asked two other minimalists who audit their apps to explain their processes. You can use their processes as inspiration for your own:

Ryan Ricketts: Minimalist, traveler, outdoorsman. - https://rickettsfish.com:

> *I find it helpful to keep my most-used apps on the first page, and my less-used apps on the second page, in folders. I also keep the bottom row of apps open to minimize visual clutter. I have no folders on my first page of apps. I'm ruthless about which apps deserve a spot on the first page. When I notice a first-page app is not being used, I move it to the second page and replace it with another.*

Jeremy Ginsburg: #EntrePerformer. Culture Chameleon. #VietNomad. - http://www.jeremyginsburg.com

Here is what I do:

1. Schedule a 30 min block.
2. Go through my apps and ask "would I pay for this if I didn't already own it?".
3. Delete willingly.
4. Go celebrate.

Both Ryan Ricketts and Jeremy Ginsburg are highly successful minimalists who have a lot to say and teach. As soon as you get tired of hearing from me, consider going to their websites to gain additional perspectives and thoughts on how other people are living life well.

Now that we have covered some tips and processes for minimizing virtual distractions, let's jump back into the real world and focus on minimizing unneeded objects.

Chapter 14: Objects

For several years of my life I owned less than 100 total belongings. This included all of my clothes, all of my electronics, and all of my other gear. The goal of this admittedly extreme lifestyle had little to do with a number and much more to do with value. Once I started counting my items, I started valuing each of them more. As I eliminated the superfluous, I gained more respect for the items I called my own. Without conscious thought, I started taking better care of my remaining objects and appreciated them more. Step by step, day by day, my emerging Minimalist Mindset started to show itself in my physical world.

Each of us is different, and thus each of us have different requirements from life. With regard to objects, there is no right number or minimum requirement. The only important metric is whatever arbitrary number you want to choose as your tool for getting more value out of the objects you choose to fill your life with.

Remember, making the conscious decision to own fewer objects is an active step toward subtracting the unnecessary from your life. The goal of minimalism with regard to objects is not to get rid of all of your things, instead it is to make room for what you truly think is important.

The process of purging extra belongings is usually viewed as the hardest part of minimalism. I think this is correct, getting rid of stuff is very difficult. A perceived sense of value led each of us to acquire things in the first place and that sense of value tends to linger. That said, it is the difficulty of this task that makes it rewarding. Once you start winning the battle over owning too many things, you will start to feel a growing sense of mental fortitude and freedom. The first manifestation of this feeling comes during the great purge.

The Great Purge

One of the great joys of becoming a minimalist is the feeling of freedom that comes from having your own great purge. The process is simple. Create four piles for all of your belongings:

1. Stuff to keep
2. Stuff to donate
3. Stuff to throw away
4. Stuff to set aside in a box

I recommend doing your great purge over the course of a weekend, but you can take as long as you want. If necessary, start with only a specific closet or room and then move on to your entire house. The process isn't about instant gratification, it is about forward progress and increasing personal freedom.

Once you have picked your initial scope, move everything out into the open. If items are stuffed in drawers, pull them out and place them in the middle of the floor. Do this for every stationary item in the room. You want to be able to plainly see all of your items. This enables you to sort them.

If all of your items do not fit on the floor within a room, subdivide the room and work on individual sections.

Once you have your items out in the open, start sorting them into the four piles mentioned before (Keep, Donate, Throw Away, Box). We will discuss what to do with each of these piles in the forthcoming sections. In the meantime, continue this process for as long as it makes sense for you.

Your own great purge will be as easy or as hard as you want it to be. (See the rest of this chapter for tips on how to deal with the pain that is associated with purging objects.) If you are not ready to make the deep plunge all at once, you can start small by putting a few items in the donate and throw away piles every day. The great purge is a process that can be repeated as many times as you want.

Many people find themselves forced to do a great purge due to a lifestyle change (e.g., new home, new job, or new relationship status). In these cases, the great purge tends to have a lot more items in the donate and throw away piles. This can be a great experience and a sign of a new way of life.

Whatever the size of your great purge you should be proud of yourself for making forward progress. Some items will be easy to purge, but undoubtedly you will encounter objects that are hard to part with. For those pesky items, you can rely on the Box Technique. For everything else, you can pat yourself on the back and be proud.

The Box Technique

Some objects are harder to get rid of than others. For me, the two hardest kind of objects to get rid of were my books (see Chapter 15: Books) and my college t-shirts (see Chapter 18: Clothing). Getting rid of the rest of the junk in my apartment was easy, but trying to get rid of those particular objects seemed jarring and shortsighted. If you start feeling that way during your purge, take a deep breath and acknowledge that you are perfectly normal. Remember to be kind to yourself. Afterward, I recommend trying the Box Technique.

For items that you just can't part with, try putting them into a box and then storing that box in a hard to reach place. You don't need to lose access to these items, you just merely need to make them less of a part of your day-to-day life. Out of sight, out of mind, but not out of your life.

If you legitimately need an item you have put in the box, you can open the box and remove it. Otherwise, the items should stay in the box.

After several months, a funny thing will start to happen: those feelings of attachment you felt toward your objects will start to naturally and painlessly disappear. It will take some time (three to six months in my experience), but this technique consistently works.

After six months or so have passed, take an honest look at the box. If you still see the contents of the box as a requirement for your life, then keep it. If not, find the contents of the box a new owner.

When I did this I was amazed at how painlessly this technique removed my former attachment to my objects. Before using the technique, my college shirts were important physical mini-monuments to the good times I had in college. I felt like discarding the shirts meant discarding the memories. After using this technique, this unhelpful link between the objects and my past experiences was extinguished. This let me appreciate the past while making room for the future.

Donation Sundays

After you have successfully completed a great purge, you will discover something odd: even though you have been removing unimportant items from your life, you will be somehow still be adding items back in without even knowing it. Maybe a friend leaves some clothes at your place, or a well-intentioned relative gives you a book. Maybe your neighbor brings you some new artwork or you mysteriously find somebody else's socks in your laundry. Whatever the source, new items will make their way into your life.

To combat this, you can use a technique called Donation Sundays. The technique is really quite self explanatory. Each Sunday, set aside a group of objects to donate. You can donate them to friends, charity, or to other people in need. By making this a habit, you become both a more helpful part of your community and you complete the maintenance that is necessary to continue to be a minimalist.

Here are two simple sub-techniques for making this happen:

- Utilize a large Donation Sunday bin or bag. Put it in your closet or garage. I find that it's easier to separate the decision to get rid of something from the decision of *how* to get rid of something. Use Donation Sunday to put things in the bin; when it fills up, use Donation Sunday to empty it.
- Periodically invite friends to go through your Donation Sunday container and take anything for free. You can do this at the end of a get-together, or on a specific Sunday afternoon every few months. As a result of using this sub-technique, my friend and fellow minimalist, Ryan Ricketts, once had his friends in tears when they took a free Xbox 360 from his donation bin for their children's birthday gift.

One Thing in, Two Things Out

Being a minimalist does not mean that you do not buy new things. Inevitably your items will break, wear out, or otherwise need replacing. In these cases you are certainly justified in buying new objects. But there is one caveat. In order to fight the influx of objects that the world is sure to send your way, you should try to donate or get rid of two things for every one thing you buy. You will likely be as surprised as I was that this technique actually results in you keeping roughly the same amount of total objects rather than forcing you toward zero. In a world that constantly pushes the new, must-have thing, you need to actively fight to stay minimal.

List Mania

While not a necessity for everyone, many people find it useful to create lists of the items they own. Having an up-to-date list of all of your belongings has several benefits:

- Going through the act of creating a list makes one aware of how much they own.
- Having a list can be valuable for insurance claims in the event that objects get destroyed or stolen.
- Having a list of items with brands, UPCs, and product models makes replacing items easier.

While your online retailer of choice may vary, I found it most convenient to structure my lists as Amazon wish lists. The advantages of this are it makes re-ordering items easy and it gives me instant access to current market value of my items.

Having already created an Amazon wish list that contains everything that I own, I know that in the event of an emergency I can reorder all of my belongings with a single click. This realization of the replaceability of my objects helps me de-prioritize them correctly.

Now that we have covered the high level techniques for paring down your objects, let's dive into the specifics of how to deal with some of your most beloved objects. We will start with books.

Chapter 15: Books

There is something magical about books. The feel of their pages, the memories associated with their stories, and the feeling of universality that they can create are all undeniably important. For almost everyone, books are the hardest objects to part with. This is perfectly acceptable.

Remember, if you choose to part ways with your books, you can go at your own pace. Depending on your priorities you can keep all of your books, give one away every Sunday (see the section "Donation Sundays" in Chapter 14: Objects), or sell your whole library to a second hand book store.

For me, the realization that allowed me to part ways with my books came after looking at the bigger picture of how physical books interacted with my life. My books were important to me, but I was able to acknowledge that they had downsides. First of all, I could use my lopsided and creaking bookshelf as evidence that my books were heavy. The idea of moving all of them and reorganizing them was daunting, and it was one of the things that was preventing me from living abroad. The second downside was that I could see they were slowly deteriorating. The oldest books on the shelf had already started to fade, and some pages had already become unreadable. This point was closely related to the thought that finally brought me to my tipping point with my books. I knew that in the event of a fire I would have no way of saving all of my books. They were simply too heavy, clunky, and fragile.

With these thoughts, I packed my books into a box (see the section "The Box Technique" in Chapter 14: Objects), cataloged them on a file on my computer (see the section "List Mania" in Chapter 14: Objects), and stored the boxes in a closet. After about six months, I thought about the replaceability of my books and finally was able to donate them to friends and a used bookstore. Releasing my books ended up being the last hurdle holding me back from moving abroad. Shortly after donating my books I moved to Buenos Aires, Argentina to start a new, more adventurous life.

Digital Clones

If you absolutely cannot part with your books, you have another option. Instead of outright getting rid of them, you can replace them with electronic versions. While you will not retain the value of being able to hold the books, you will gain the benefits that are associated with electronic books (weightless, search-ability, natural disaster proofing, global accessibility). This way you can keep the story without having to deal with the physical weight and mind-space of the tangible book.

Amazon offers a discount on many e-books as long as they can verify that you purchased the physical copy from their online store. This is a great way to enjoy the feeling of the book without having to worry about the storage of the book after you finish it. In some cases, I use this technique to read a physical book, buy the e-version, and then give the physical book to a friend who I think will enjoy it.

Regardless of what you decide to do with your books, remember that you can move at your own speed. Becoming a minimalist does not necessarily require fast action, although, like removing a Band-Aid, sometimes fast action can be easier in the long-term. The Minimalist Mindset is more of a destination than a journey, it is up to you on how you want to get there.

Chapter 16: Photos

After books, physical photos are generally the hardest objects for people to shed. Paradoxically, they are also the type of object that has the greatest benefits when replaced with digital copies.

From Analog to Digital

While it is true that there is something special about the feel of old photos, the benefits digital conversion offers over traditional photos is overwhelming. First and foremost, tangible photos irreversibly degrade over time. Even without the legitimate dangers of fire, floods, and loss, perfectly safe photos will slowly disintegrate and degrade in color quality over time. This process is irreversible (unless corrected in a digital form!) and completely preventable.

Modern scanners and free phone apps can inexpensively scan photos in incredibly high resolution. The resulting digital replacements are more flexible than the originals and don't suffer from any of the aforementioned concerns of physical photos.

Photo Scanning Party (or Not!)

While much easier than in the past, photo scanning still takes a fair amount of manual work. There are two popular solutions to this problem.

The first solution is to throw a photo scanning party. These work parties are pretty simple. Multiple people get together and help each other digitize shared physical photos. These events are great for swapping stories and reminiscing about the past. The host and attendees simply use free smartphone apps (which in my experience provide unexpectedly good results) or buy or rent easy-to-use scanners, and then split the cost so that they can share resources and scan all of the photos of the people in attendance. Normally this takes place over several events. The resulting digital photos can then be shared between the group and saved onto file sharing cloud services.

If a photo scanning party sounds terrible to you, don't panic, you have other options. There are plenty of professional services that will gladly accept your physical photos, film, cassettes, CDs, DVDs, and other old media for digital conversion. I was very resistant to this idea at first, as I didn't want to risk losing my original copies. In my case, I wanted to digitize film based videos and I wanted to save old photos that were stored on a crumbling CD. These items stored priceless childhood moments. I tried to do the conversion myself but quickly realized that I couldn't do it in a cost effective way. Eventually I made the leap to pay for a professional service. Less than a week later, I received a link to all of my newly digitized photos and videos. I was incredibly happy with the results, as I was previously sure that my crumbling CD with priceless photos was too far degraded to save. Happily, the equipment the professional service used was able to read the old CD and digitize the obscure film formats with ease.

The process is straightforward. You simply mail in your objects (sometimes in a prepaid shipping box), and they scan and store the digital conversions and then mail you back the physical originals. The biggest benefit to these services (other than the convenience) is that many of these services utilize higher quality scanners, VCRs, and disk readers than are practical for an individual to own.

See https://www.lifelisted.com/min for up-to-date recommendations on photo scanning devices, apps, and professional services.

Backup Solutions

Once you convert your photos to digital form, you need somewhere to store them. Depending on your circumstance, you could store them on hard drives at your home, in the cloud online, or both simultaneously. There is a disagreement in the online minimalist community about which is the better practice. Some minimalists argue that the cloud is safe enough and that storing them at home adds unnecessary electronic equipment to your life. Others argue that solely storing your priceless memories in the cloud is dangerous and not safe enough. I agree with the latter groups (store them in two places), but understand where the other group is coming from. In the end, the best solution is the one that works best for your specific circumstance and goals.

There are plenty of backup services available, but they are not all the same. To find the best option you should consider price, storage space offered, speed of file transfer, and backup solution for the cloud provider itself.

See https://www.lifelisted.com/min for up-to-date recommendations on cloud storage and backup services.

Displaying Digital Photos

While you can just digitize your photos and then upload them to the cloud, it is a lot more practical to take the extra step and actually display them. I have found the best option for this is to use either a TV screensaver-like app, or a single purpose digital photo frame. The advantage of the single purpose device is that these kind of devices, unlike traditional photo frames, can cycle through many photos and adjust the photo they are showing based on changing contexts.

See https://www.lifelisted.com/min for recommendations on photo displays.

Shifting your physical photos (and videos) to digital versions gives you a whole host of advantages (mainly durability and transferability) but it can cause a new problem. How do you deal with all of these new computer files? We will cover this modern problem in the next chapter.

Chapter 17: Computers

Computer files are not tangible, but they certainly take up mind-space and hard drive space. In aggregate, clicking around the folders on your computer while looking for a file adds up to a significant amount of time that you could otherwise spend doing something that you love. While there are literally bookshelves full of books that have been written about digital organization, we are going to keep to the theme and focus on the best minimalist techniques.

One Project = One Folder

Every project has two types of items, action items and resources. Action items are the tasks that you actually need to do (e.g., "Reserve camping site") while resources are the non-task items that are directly related to completing a task. (e.g., a map of local camping sites.) You can use whatever organizational system you want for organizing tasks, but the one thing you should do is make a simple connection for tying your action items to related resources.

My favorite way of doing this is using the simplest naming scheme possible by just consistently using the name of the project.

For example, pretend I am organizing the camping trip that was mentioned earlier. The moment I start the project I would take two actions. First I would create a folder on my computer called "July Camping Trip". I would then create a to-do list with the same name, "July Camping Trip" to store my action items. Using the same name for both the resources folder and to-do list makes it very simple to identify how resources and action items fit together.

To be clear, the folder you create could be digital or tangible; the correct option is what works best for your lifestyle. Similarly, the to-do list could be digital (Evernote, Omnifocus, Todoist, etc), or it could physical (a notepad, Moleskin notebook, etc). Again, the best practice is the option that works best for you.

Organizing your projects this way is simple and cuts down on the time and energy needed to mentally associate and find related tasks and resources.

Store Everything in the Cloud

Computers get stolen, hard drives fail, and important luggage gets lost. It is part of life, and largely unavoidable. The best thing you can do to mitigate these risks is to store your files in the cloud. The biggest benefit to this is you don't need to have as much local storage space, which means you can eliminate or minimize the amount of hard drives you have to own and carry.

The best implementations of consumer focused clouds are those where the files are stored locally on your device and synced to the cloud. This enables you to have access to your files even when you don't have Internet access. Happily, there are a multitude of popular and secure cloud options that are set up this way. See https://www.lifelisted.com/min under the title "Cloud Services" for an up-to-date list of the best options.

If you choose to store your files in the cloud, it is important to keep your online cloud accounts secure. Currently the best and easiest way to do this is to enable Two Factor Authentication (free on practically all major consumer cloud providers). Enabling this makes it so that in addition to your username and password, a temporary code that is only available on your trusted devices (usually a mobile phone) is required to access your account. This means that if someone was able to hack and extract your username and password they would still need physical access to your trusted device in order to access your files.

Storing your data in the cloud allows you to shed excess external hard drives and perhaps more importantly, the stress and fear that goes along with storing your files in only one spot.

Passwords

I hate passwords! They are annoying and mediocre at their primary purpose, security. According to a Telesign Consumer Account Security Report[16] that was compiled using 2,000 consumers in the US and UK:

- 73% of accounts are guarded by duplicate passwords (passwords shared among two or more accounts).
- 47% of people use passwords that are at least 5 years old.

Given the amount of accounts that are breached

every year, old and reused passwords are huge security risks. In addition to being poor security devices, passwords are a constant annoyance that modern computer users must retype multiple times a day. They are largely ineffective, and in aggregate use a lot of valuable time.

Unfortunately, they are also necessary. The vast majority of online accounts require them.

The best method for minimizing passwords has two components:

1. Have fewer online accounts
2. Utilize encrypted password managers

The first method is easy. Fewer online accounts equals less risk. Take an opportunity at least once a year to deactivate old accounts (notable offenders are accounts from old jobs and old relationships). In addition to decreasing your chances of getting hacked, this exercise decreases the amount of accounts that send you unwanted e-mail.

The second method of minimizing password waste is also easy. Simply use an encrypted password manager to manage unique passwords for every online account you have. The advantages of using one of these systems are it makes it feasible to have hundreds of different passwords, and the manager itself can audit your passwords to alert you about duplicates and passwords that are old and should be replaced.

See https://www.lifelisted.com/min for my current recommendations on password managers.

Chapter 18: Clothing

You do not need to be a nudist to be a minimalist! Minimalism is about living more with less, but it doesn't mean living without anything. Clothes are absolutely essential. Counterintuitively, they are also worth minimizing.

Clothes are instrumental in the first impressions you make upon others and they are key to living a healthy and productive life. Since different items of clothing can express different messages and serve different functions, it is a natural tendency to prepare for every possible situation with an overabundance of clothing. This is problematic for at least one not so obvious reason.

Full closets require a whole lot of mental energy to

utilize and maintain. How often have you asked yourself what you were going to wear on a given day? For those of us who do not dress other people for a living, this question uses creative energy that could otherwise be used on more worthwhile tasks. How often have you looked at your closet and felt a twinge of stress concerning your complicated clothing options? This stress will continue to exist every day if you don't do something about it.

So what can you do about the all to common problem of owning too much clothing? The answer, like many problems, is to minimize.

There are two requirements for minimizing your wardrobe:

1. Specifically identify your clothing requirements.
2. Take actions to make your clothes work harder for you.

I'll warn you, while the following process will make purging your clothing easier, it will still be a difficult plunge to take. Clothing has a lot of sentimental value. For most people, clothing, photos and books are the three hardest items to purge. Like most improvements in life though, the hardest tasks offer the greatest rewards.

Above all, remember the best fashion is not

clothing, it is confidence. Confidence looks great on everybody.

Identify Your Clothing Requirements

Ready to not be surprised? People living in the arctic require different clothing compared to people living in a hot desert. Similarly, a fashionista living in New York requires different clothing than a nomadic adventurer. As such, your task as a minimalist is to identify your specific clothing requirements. To do this, start by asking yourself these questions:

- What clothing do you wear the most often?
- What clothing have you not worn in over six months?
- What clothing have you not worn in over twelve months?
- What clothing has extreme sentimental value to you?
- What are your work clothing requirements?
- What are your social clothing requirements?

Take some time, mine your closet or drawers, and be honest with yourself. You need to think through these questions before you can be successful with the actions that follow.

Take Actions to Make Your Clothes Work Harder for You

After you have answered those questions, it is time to take action! The process will be very similar to the process discussed earlier in Chapter 14: Objects.

First Round Clothing Purge

This step is both fun and scary. First, create four big piles:

1. Keep
2. Donate
3. Trash
4. Box

Your first action is to take out all of the clothing you own and spread it out over an open space. Free your clothing from the crevices of your drawers and unreachable corners of your closets. The odds are high that you own clothing that you don't even know about. You want to see your whole wardrobe out in the open.

After you have freed your clothing and gazed upon your collection, it is time to start sorting.

Start by taking all of the clothing that you wear the most often and putting them into the "Keep" pile.

(Keep in mind that this may include clothing that is in your laundry bin. If that is the case, put that clothing in a separate bag and add that bag to the "Keep" pile.)

Next, take all of your extremely sentimental clothing (wedding dresses, high school jerseys, family heirlooms, etc.) and put them in your "Box" pile. Don't worry, you will be keeping these items too! See the section on "The Box Technique" in Chapter 14: Objects for more information.

Next, take all of the clothing that you have not worn in 12 months[17] and put them in the "Trash" or "Donate" piles. If you have seasonal items (like snow clothes) that you haven't worn in a year but are not yet ready to get rid of, put those in the "Box" pile.

This will leave you with the clothing that you have not worn in the last six months. Now you are at the hard part. Think back to the six questions you asked yourself earlier about your clothing requirements. Remember what is absolutely required of your clothing from work and your community. What can you do without? Remember, extra clothing fills up more than your drawers and closets, it also takes up valuable space in your mind. Start paring down these clothes by sorting these items between your "Donate", "Box", and "Trash" piles.

This process usually takes a long time. Take the time to enjoy the process as much as possible. Digging through old clothes typically brings up old memories. Take time to appreciate both the good and the bad memories. Clothing is very personal and very important to both how we see ourselves and how others see us.

At some point in this process you are likely to find a piece of clothing that you have not yet worn and are thus unable to get rid of it. When this happens, do the following:

1. Think about how the clothing made you feel when you bought it.
2. Thank the clothing for that feeling (you can do this in your head if other people are around, but don't skip this step!)
3. Acknowledge that the clothing has served its purpose by granting you that feeling.
4. Put the article of clothing in the "Donate" pile.

Remember, past purchase decisions do not need to control your ability to minimize in the present. Appreciate (or laugh at) your prior self and take action to build a better, more simplified life going forward.

After a lot of hard work on your part, you should reach a point where all of your clothing is sorted into four large piles.

Take the items in your "Keep" pile and put them back in your closets and/or drawers[18].

Take the items in your "Donate" pile, put them in bags and set a time on your calendar to donate those items. You can donate these either to a charity or to friends. The important part though is that you schedule a time to do this and stick to it. You do not want to continue to store these items.

Next, take the items in the "Trash" pile and put them into bags or boxes. Take the time, right now if possible, to actually put these in the trash. You want to be rid of these things as quickly as possible.

This should leave you with only the items in your "Box" pile. See the section titled "The Box Technique" in Chapter 14: Objects for instructions on what to do with these items.

Consolidating Clothing Brands/Types

The single most powerful action you can take to simplify your clothing is to consolidate brands and types. The normal wardrobe is like a patchwork quilt. People tend to have a multitude of types and styles of socks, shirts, and underwear. While diversity can be good, in the case of clothing it can also be an unnecessary pain.

Consider the common chore of sorting your socks after doing laundry. This task is never finished (like laundry itself) and adds very little value to your life relative to the amount of time it takes. Now imagine if you had just two styles of socks, casual socks and business socks. Pretend the casual socks are all the same and the business socks are all the same. If this were the case, think about how easy and fast sorting would become! All of the casual socks would be interchangeable and all of the business socks would be interchangeable. Sorting would only take seconds and would clear up time for you to use your mind for tasks that are actually important.

You can do the same for your underwear and certain types of accessories (pantyhose, cuff links, etc).

But what about shirts and pants? Narrowing these down to one color and style is overkill for most people. Instead, focus on consolidating brand and fit but not color or style. If you find a shirt that fits you perfectly, buy it in several colors and styles. Likewise, if you find a pair of jeans that fit you just right, consider buying a couple pairs from the same brand. (This is of course to replace your other clothes.) You certainly don't have to replace all of your clothes with a single brand and style (you are not a robot), but you should focus on condensing your wardrobe.

Still skeptical? Consider how doing this might positively impact your life. How long and how much creative energy do you spend in the morning deciding what to wear? How much time do you spend sorting laundry? Even if it is not a lot during any individual session, the amount of time, and more importantly, the amount of mental energy, that those sessions take up in aggregate will likely add up to entire days of your life. This is time and energy that is right there waiting for you to reclaim.

Schedule Recurring Mini-Purges

Nobody expects you to be an extreme minimalist alien robot! You do not have to eliminate all of your stuff in one go, doing so would be insane and incredibly stressful. Instead, it is much more healthy and reasonable to do one big purge and then schedule mini-purges going forward. I recommend doing small purges every Sunday. See the section titled "Donation Sundays" in Chapter 14: Objects for more information.

Doing these recurring purges also has the added benefit of fighting the inevitable creep of new clothing that somehow makes its way into all of our lives. Being a minimalist is not simply an act done once, it is a constant art and lifestyle that requires maintenance. This attribute of continuity is one of the key differences between the idea of minimalism and the Minimalist Mindset.

Minimalist Men's Clothing List

The following is an example of my wardrobe. Your

life context will likely be different than mine but use this list as a starting point and customize it to your own clothing requirements:

- 8 pairs of one style everyday socks (for me, this is only business appropriate socks)
- 6 pairs of one style workout socks
- 8 pairs of one style of underwear
- 3 pairs of shoes (athletic, everyday, dress)
- 2 pairs of jeans
- 1 pair of all purpose shorts
- 2 workout shirts
- 2 workout shorts
- 6 t-shirts
- 1 belt
- 1 all purpose jacket
- 3 long sleeve shirts
- A hatred of specialized clothing (suits, swimsuits, gear, gross!)

Minimalist Women's Clothing List

If you are female, use the following list as a starting point and customize your list[19] to your own clothing requirements.

- 6 pairs of one style everyday socks
- 3 pairs of one style workout socks

- 6 pairs of one style of underwear/bras
- 3 pairs of shoes (athletic, everyday, dress)
- 2 workout shirts
- 2 workout shorts
- 1 all purpose shorts
- 2 coats (1 heavy and 1 light)
- 1 sweater
- 2 blouses
- 3 t-shirts
- 1 belt
- 2 pairs of jeans
- 1 pair of trousers
- 1 all purpose dress ("Little Black Dress")
- A hatred of specialized clothing (suits, swimsuits, gear, gross!)

Now that we have covered the specific task of minimizing clothing let's move on to something more big picture, minimalist travel.

Chapter 19: Travel

For me, travel is the main reason why I make minimalism-related sacrifices in my life. In order to facilitate travel I implement a lifestyle I dub "Living Out of My Ferrari." Most people in the developed world spend the majority of their income on Rent/Mortgage, Transportation, Food, Health Care/Insurance, and Entertainment (in that order). If they have money left over, they use that cash for vacationing. This is the norm, but there *is* an alternative.

Many people who are part of the minimalism movement (myself included) spend their money on travel first and the more traditional expense areas second. Like a homeless but car-obsessed person living out of a Ferrari, many minimalists have the reversed priorities of most people and live an unconventional, travel-centered lifestyle. They make large sacrifices in areas where money is commonly spent (not owning or renting a home for example) but as a result are able to live travel-centered lifestyles that are normally reserved for the ultra rich.

(Almost) Always Stick with One Airline/Hotel Program

Here is an important travel spoiler alert for you. Most airlines are essentially identical. Yes some will have luxurious perks and others will be extremely uncomfortable, but all of the airlines will get you from point A to point B by selling you a ticket to sit in a large flying tube. At the time of writing, the majority of commercial airlines conduct most of their flights on Airbus A320/A330/A340s or Boeing 737s. The vast majority of airplanes in the sky right this moment are essentially clones of each other. Airlines can diversify their offerings in services but all of the international airlines worldwide are severely limited by governmental regulations.

You can choose to obsess over which airline offers in-seat plugs or which has the funniest advertising campaigns, or you can get over these tiny differences and focus on your destination.

Since all commercial flights are very similar, I

recommend (almost) always sticking with one airline. This enables you to make the most out of a single mileage program, and maximizing the amount of free flights and upgrades that you can get. (To find the best airline for you, research which airline has the most direct flights from your home airport.)

There is one major exception to this. It never makes sense to spend vastly more on your favorite airline for the sake of earning points when there is an equivalent flight that costs a lot less money. On average, individual airline points are equal to roughly one cent USD (with very heavy inflation). If you spend vastly more on a flight in order to earn miles you have effectively lost money and given free money to the airlines (this is why mileage programs are profitable for airlines to begin with).

The same idea (but to a lesser degree) is true for hotels. Hotels, motels, and apartment rentals vary much more in their diversity of offerings, locations, and services as compared to airlines but they are still largely the same at a base level (they all offer a room that is meant for sleeping). When economical, it is best to stick with one hotel reward program so that you can maximize your points earning potential. At the same time, the points are not usually the goal worth optimizing for, instead it is better to optimize for better lodging in general. With lodging, I always aim to balance price (or point value) with distance to the destinations I care about. Utilizing cheap lodging is great unless you are going to need to pay a fortune in transportation costs to actually get where you plan on going.

Stick to as few airline and hotel reward programs as possible, but don't fool yourself into thinking that earning points is the end goal. Instead, remember it is the inherent rewards of travel that are valuable, not the artificial point systems.

Don't Repeat Locations

We live in an incredibly diverse and rapidly changing world. While it is a more simplistic option to repeat travel locations, this attractive tendency unintentionally dilutes the value of travel.

Traveling is a tremendously powerful educational tool because it enables you to learn about yourself by experiencing worldviews that are different from your own. For many people, it is the feeling of being stuck in a routine back home that drives them to travel.

While it certainly makes sense to have some favorite travel locations (like an easy to get to weekend getaway), try to diversify your travels as much as possible. If you travel to a specific place multiple times, you run the high risk of falling into a new routine there. These transported routines limit your ability to experience a new worldview and thus take away from the value of travel. Going to a resort for the 8th time is still technically traveling but it isn't normally as beneficial for you as going to a new country. Fight this easy mistake and make the effort to expand your world rather than simply duplicating it.

It Is Not about Proximity, It Is about Power

There is a major misconception in modern society that the best travel destinations are the ones that are farthest away. Foreign does not need to mean far away. Sometimes, the best trips can be those where you play tourist in your own town.

The only important requirement of traveling is to experience something new to you.

The proximity to your home is not important. Instead, the most important part of traveling is the power of experiencing a new situation or worldview. Don't let distance or resources prevent you from traveling. If you can't fly, drive. If you can't drive, walk. Regardless of how you do it, minimize what is unimportant and maximize your travel experiences.

Never Fully Unpack

Traveling is hard. It requires you to experience the unknown and to adapt to confusing and foreign situations. While I strongly believe that the benefits of travel outweigh these downsides, it is important to acknowledge that traveling is difficult. As with anything that is difficult, this hurdle creates a very real barrier to entry.

I have found that the best way to lower the barrier to entry to traveling is to simply never fully unpack. If you are already partially packed for a trip, it makes it that much easier to get there.

In practical terms, this means keeping your travel specific items in your suitcase (passport, travel accessories, some clothing). This small step can make traveling seem surprisingly less daunting. If you are already packed, you are already partly ready to go.

The Minimalist Packing List

The following is the minimalist packing list[20] that I use as a baseline for all of my travels. This list overlaps with the "Minimalist Clothing List" that is in Chapter 18: Clothing. Feel free to use this as a guide to creating your own personalized minimalist packing list.

- Roller Case (Cases with four smart wheels are the most convenient)
- Ear plugs
- Travel toothbrush/paste/floss
- Nail clippers

- Extra waterproof garbage/sandwich bags (for storing other items)
- USB thumb drive
- Pen
- Universal power adapter
- Laminated vaccination documentation
- Credit cards
- Passport
- Applicable clothes (see Chapter 18: Clothing)

Remember, the goal is cover your essential travel needs without bringing extraneous gear. If in doubt, leave something out. For many items, you can buy them at your destination.

Chapter 20: Gifts

 Gifts are one of the most impactful ways people can show their gratitude for other people. By both demonstrating empathy by knowing what someone may want, and by showing devotion by actually sacrificing in order to purchase or create the applicable gift, people are able to express important feelings through gifting. Unfortunately, gifts also have a downside. Gifts are usually objects that are not chosen by their owners and are unusually difficult to part with. Gifts generally have good intentions behind them, but they are not always entirely helpful for someone seeking freedom or the Minimalist Mindset.

 Happily, there are techniques you can use to experience the upsides of gifting while minimizing the downsides.

Give Gifts the Way You Want to Receive Gifts

The first technique for effective minimalist gifting is to give gifts as you would like to receive them. The following are my favorite minimalist gifts to both give and receive:

- **The gift of your time** - This can either be personal (like when you go out of your way to listen to someone who is normally not heard) or professional (like when you gift your professional services to someone in need).
- **The gift of shared events** - My favorite personal traditional is to spend New Year's Eve in a foreign country with friends and family. By far the most important and rewarding part of these trips is seeing unconnected friends of mine become connected with each other through shared experiences. My gift to them is organizing the event and their gift to me is sharing the experience with me and the other friends and family who are attending.
- **The gift of experiences** - Rather than give my family and friends physical gifts, I give them the gifts of experiences. Sometimes these are

simple and inexpensive like going to a new park together, other times they are more elaborate like going on a cruise together. These gifts are always winners and I have had multiple friends confirm to me that these gifted experiences are more important and more appreciated than any physical gift they have ever received.

The golden rule says, "Treat others like you would like to be treated." One concrete action you can take is to apply this important rule to your gifts. Take the rewards you gain from the Minimalist Mindset and give them to your loved ones. In doing so, your gifts will stand out and likely be more appreciated than typical gifts.

Make Your Gift Receiving Intentions Clear

The best thing you can do to raise your chances of getting better gifts is by being more clear with what you want to be gifted. Start by having a conversation (generally around birthdays or other special events where gifts are given) with your loved ones about only wanting to receive certain kinds of gifts. Some of the best gifts are also some of the most simple:

- Time with loved ones

- Shared events/experiences with loved ones
- Travel with loved ones
- Gift cards
- Cash

Time

As mentioned in the previous section, the gift of time can be one of the most rewarding and valuable gifts of all. Anyone can give a physical item, but only you can give your time. This is true for others as well. Consider asking for an afternoon with a loved one rather than a new toy or gadget.

Shared Events/Experiences

Due to its importance, this item was also mentioned in the previous section. Shared events (group get-togethers and group adventures) are gifts that keep on giving. Unlike physical items, good memories are special in that they provide value each time they are noticed. Better yet, shared events and experiences work in a one-to-many fashion, which means you can organize just one event and you can gift it to many people you care about.

Travel

Like shared experiences, travel can have a long lasting impact as a gift. See Chapter 19: Travel for more details.

Gift Cards

Gift cards have one major advantage over cash, they can be purchased for less than they are worth. Wait until the holiday season and then scout out deals (typically online) for gift cards to big brands that are being sold for less than their value. Big consumer electronics stores, for example, will annually have sales where they sell Apple iTunes gift cards at 85% their value. This means a gift card that you spend $8.50 on is actually worth $10.00 when redeemed for iTunes products. You can find similar deals for many different brands and stores.

Cash

The flexibility of cash is hard to beat. The gift of cash can help people solve all kinds of problems. Don't ignore cash as a good option for minimalist gifts (both giving and receiving).

This section covered great minimalist gifts to both give and receive, but what are you supposed to do with the unwanted gifts that you receive?

Getting Rid of Unwanted Gifts

Getting rid of unwanted gifts is the hardest part of minimalist gifting. Gifts, more than other items, hold sentimental value. Getting rid of these items can feel like an insult to the person who gifted them.

While I don't know of a perfect solution to this problem, the best option I have found for dealing with this is to use the Box Technique as described in Chapter 14: Objects, and using the experience to note that I must do a better job of setting expectations in the future. Like all aspects of the Minimalist Mindset, gifting is always a work in progress.

Gifts, no matter how expensive they are, can not be valuable unless you are healthy enough to enjoy them. In the next two chapters we will move onto some of the most critical elements of life, food, and exercise.

Chapter 21: Food

Food is humanity's most important tool. It expresses culture, it harbors thoughtful communication, it expresses love, and it brings people together. Food is vital for all forms of life and is an essential element to a life well lived.

Food is also very expensive and time consuming to prepare and eat. While food shouldn't be overly optimized, it should be thoughtful and deliberate.

Fuel Meals

Sometimes the main purpose of a meal is to spend time with other people. Other times the purpose of a meal is to share a common experience. Many times though, the purpose of a meal is just to absorb fuel. In these times it is helpful to have what I call a *fuel meal*, a simple and standardized meal.

Fuel meals are intentionally easy to prepare and quick to eat. They are not meant to replace all of your meals. They are just meant to be an efficient way of eating when the meal doesn't need to serve a greater purpose. They won't make up all of your meals, but they might make up the bulk of them. The quantity will depend on your lifestyle. While I was writing this book I had *fuel meals* for breakfast and lunch every weekday. When I am traveling they make up only one meal a day. Still other times in my life, such as during the holidays, they are not needed at all.

Your particular diet and portion size for your *fuel meal* will vary based on your circumstances. For me, I aim for organic vegetables and easy to prepare proteins. This generally consists of frozen organic broccoli and local organic lean chicken. This is a meal I can make in ten minutes or less and I don't have to use much brain power to prepare it well.

Your *fuel meal* will vary from mine. It will be based off of what ingredients you have available to you, your budget, your cooking setup, your location, and your dietary restrictions. The recipe itself doesn't matter, the important part is that you plan for a meal that is:

- Nutritious
- Inexpensive
- Easy and fast to prepare
- Fast to eat
- Easy and fast to clean up

Remember, these *fuel meals* are not meant to replace your other important meals, they are merely meant to cut down on the time and money otherwise used on having to prepare a meal from scratch everyday.

Simple Food

Many times the best and most tasty food is simple food. If you are trying to live with a Minimalist Mindset, you should aim to make the ingredients that go into building your body as simple as possible.

When feasible, it is best to choose food that is organic, local, and unprocessed. Aside from the ethical and health benefits of these types of food, you also get the benefits of food that has less "extra stuff" in it. Although not always the case, simple food tends to be easier to process for the human body. This gives you more energy to direct toward the pursuits that you find fulfilling.

Food intake will be highly contextual and largely based on your required energy output. That said, the

World Health Organization (WHO) does offer simple food recommendations[21] that you can use as a baseline for your own diet:

For Adults

A healthy diet contains:

- Fruits, vegetables, legumes (e.g. lentils, beans), nuts, and whole grains (e.g. unprocessed maize, millet, oats, wheat, brown rice)
- At least 400 g (five portions) of fruits and vegetables a day. Potatoes, sweet potatoes, cassava, and other starchy roots are not classified as fruits or vegetables
- Less than 10% of total energy intake from free sugars, which is equivalent to 50 g (or around 12 level teaspoons) for a person of healthy body weight consuming approximately 2000 calories per day, but ideally less than 5% of total energy intake for additional health benefits. Most free sugars are added to foods or drinks by the manufacturer, cook, or consumer, and can also be found in sugars naturally present in honey, syrups, fruit juices, and fruit-juice concentrates.
- Less than 30% of total energy intake from fats. Unsaturated fats (e.g. found in fish, avocado,

nuts, sunflower, canola and olive oils) are preferable to saturated fats (e.g. found in fatty meat, butter, palm and coconut oil, cream, cheese, ghee, and lard). Industrial trans fats (found in processed food, fast food, snack food, fried food, frozen pizza, pies, cookies, margarine and spreads) are not part of a healthy diet.
- Less than 5 g of salt (equivalent to approximately 1 teaspoon) per day, and use iodized salt

For Infants and Young Children

In the first two years of a child's life, optimal nutrition fosters healthy growth and improves cognitive development. It also reduces the risk of becoming overweight or obese and developing noncommunicable diseases (NCDs) later in life.

Advice from the WHO on a healthy diet for infants and children is similar to that for adults, but the following elements are also important.

- Infants should be breastfed exclusively during the first six months of life.
- Infants should be breastfed continuously until two years of age and beyond.
- From six months of age, breast milk should be

supplemented with a variety of adequate, safe, and nutrient dense complementary foods. Salt and sugars should not be added to complementary foods.

My takeaway from reading the WHO recommendations was that much less food is required for the human body than is implied in western culture. Use the WHO recommendations as a baseline for your own simple diet and then adjust it to your personal requirements.

Drink Water

Water might be the one true miracle drug. In addition to hydrating, lubricating, and helping to regulate body temperature, water is typically inexpensive, portable, and a multipurpose tool.

The Centers for Disease Control (CDC) states even more advantages of regular water consumption[22]:

- Lubricate and cushion joints
- Protect your spinal cord and other sensitive tissues
- Get rid of wastes through urination, perspiration, and bowel movements

If none of those benefits persuade you to drink

water more regularly, consider the major effect of not drinking water:

- Death

There is only one major problem with not drinking any water, and it is very important! As you already know, not drinking water will eventually kill you. Clearly you cannot go without water, but that doesn't stop far too many of us from drinking the wrong amount of water.

So how much water should one drink?

According to Aaron E. Carroll, a professor of pediatrics at Indiana University School of Medicine in an article he wrote for the New York Times[23], society has lied to you, 8 cups is not necessary.

Many food scientists believe that the mythical requirement for 8 cups of water a day came from a 1945 Food and Nutrition Board recommendation that said people need about 2.5 liters (roughly eight cups) of water a day. The problem with the typical understanding of this statement is it fails to account for the sentence that followed closely after that recommendation. That later sentence read, "Most of this quantity is contained in prepared foods."

Water is contained within the vast majority of the food that people eat on a regular basis. Fruits, vegetables, most snacks, and drinks all contain water. Obviously water intake will be closely tied to water output, and for most people in common situations drinking eight cups of water a day won't hurt them, but it is also not strictly necessary. You can get plenty of water from the other food that you are eating.

But what if you want to supplement your food intake with extra water?

The easiest way to drink more water is to carry it around with you. The simple act of keeping water with you will remind you to drink it. I do this by carrying around a Nalgene bottle full of water and a quarter of a lemon. The Nalgene water bottle is easily washable which means I can avoid wasteful plastic bottles, and the lemon adds enough taste to the water to keep it intriguing.

If carrying a water bottle with you is not an option, make a point to replace your existing daily beverages with water.

Instead of soda with meals, choose water. It will save you money and has fewer unnecessary ingredients and calories. Instead of ordering your normal coffee, consider ordering an Americano (espresso and water). Like everything else important in life, small improvements to your lifestyle can make enormous differences in aggregate.

Eight cups of water only consumed as pure water might not be strictly necessary, but adding more hydration to your life is likely a beneficial habit to start.

The Unfair Relationship Between Food and Exercise

When it comes to losing weight or otherwise getting into better shape, there is a drastically unfair relationship between the effects of food and the effects of exercise.

You cannot out-exercise your mouth.

Simply put, food has overwhelming leverage over exercise. Millions of years of evolution have given us bodies that are remarkably efficient at converting food into energy. Simultaneously, the same processes have given us bodies that use a relatively small amount of energy to accomplish a lot. This discrepancy is the root of all modern diet complaints. Food intake has a seemingly disproportionate impact on getting into better shape than does exercise.

To illustrate this, imagine a 155 pound (70.31 kg) person who just ate a large Big Mac Combo with a Coke from McDonald's.
According to the nutritional facts published by McDonald's[24], and the established calories burned by activity as published by Harvard Medical School[25], that person would need to walk 15.75 miles (25.35 km)

to burn off that meal. (This assumes a 17 min/mi pace.)

Even more striking, the same person would need to run over 11 miles (17.7 km) to burn off the same meal. (This assumes a 8 min/mi pace.)

This discrepancy between the ease of taking in calories and the difficulty of burning calories is alarming. As such, if your goal is weight loss, your discipline with food will need to be far higher than your discipline with exercise. You need both to succeed, but your efforts are better spent minimizing excess calorie intake rather than focusing on calorie burning activities.

Food is a tremendous resource for human beings. The great power that food holds over us is the reason we need to give it the respect it deserves. Being present and active about the role food plays in your life is key to the Minimalist Mindset. You don't always have to minimize your food (it has many cultural and physiological benefits that can be maximized) but you do need to take it seriously.

Chapter 22: Exercise

The human body is inconceivably complex. Each of our individual cells are intricate machines that work together as tiny pieces of a much grander machine that we call our bodies. As such, keeping our bodies operating efficiently and effectively is an incredibly hard and complicated task.

People almost unanimously agree that diet and exercise are important for keeping us healthy, but as a society we have not yet figured out what is the optimal method or routine. Each of us have different needs and goals for our bodies, and as such there is no one exercise regimen that will be optimal for everyone. Therefore, instead of striving for optimal rules, it is more reasonable to follow general principles. Below are a few exercise practices that will help you be minimalistic and healthy.

Walks

One of the first abilities that separated human beings from other animals was our ability to stand upright and walk. This ability is core to who we are as a species and is one of our greatest advantages.

The benefits of taking walks are numerous and amazing. The American Heart Association states[26] that walking for at least 30 minutes a day can help do all of the following:

- Reduce the risk of coronary heart disease
- Improve blood pressure and blood sugar levels
- Improve blood lipid profile
- Maintain body weight and lower the risk of obesity
- Enhance mental well being
- Reduce the risk of osteoporosis
- Reduce the risk of breast and colon cancer
- Reduce the risk of non-insulin dependent (type 2) diabetes

Walking can be done almost anywhere, has a low dropout rate, and unlike a lot of other popular workouts, has a relatively low impact on your joints.

The World Health Organization (WHO) recommends adults aged 18–64 should do at least 150 minutes of moderate-intensity aerobic physical activity throughout the week (or do at least 75 minutes of vigorous-intensity aerobic physical activity throughout the week or an equivalent combination of moderate- and vigorous-intensity activity).[27] If you choose to go walking to reach these levels, the habit is easy to implement, requires no extra equipment, and has disproportionately high benefits to the amount of effort required.

Here's a list of easy ways you can work walking into your daily schedule:

- Walk to work
- Walk to some or all of your appointments
- Walk with a friend that you have been meaning to catch up with
- Instead of meeting for coffee or tea, have a walking meeting with a colleague or co-worker
- Walk to lunch
- Walk while listening to music, an audiobook or a podcast
- Walk right after dinner to help you digest your meal
- Take a quick walk first thing in the morning to wake yourself up without caffeine

As mentioned, walking has a lot of benefits but it is not itself a catch-all for exercise. In order to lose weight and push our bodies in a positive way, we need to place stress on our bodies from time to time. Not work-related mental stress, but reasonable physical stress. To accomplish this extra push, consider adding a minimalist workout to your day.

Minimalist Workouts

While walking is an excellent minimalist workout, it is not perfect for everybody. Every person's body is different and every body has different needs. While there are a countless amount of possible workouts, the ones that tend to be the most effective have both of the following traits:

- Being an exercise that you will actually do
- Being an exercise that actually creates positive change in *your* body

Finding these kinds of exercises is easier than many assume.

The first trait is most easily accomplished by identifying extremely simple exercises that do not require additional equipment. Some of my favorite are:

- Walking
- Running
- Jumping
- Push-ups
- Sit-ups
- Squats
- Climbers
- Burpees
- Lunges

(While these exercises are relatively simple to perform, for the sake of safety and effectiveness, it is best to verify your form with a trained professional and to check with your doctor before performing these exercises. Nothing is more effective at stopping a workout habit than an injury.)

The second trait of an effective workout is more difficult to identify. Since every body is different, finding your match will require trial and error. The best way to do this is by trying lots of different exercises and then comparing the results within your own body.

See https://www.lifelisted.com/min for up-to-date recommendations on minimalist workout routines and exercises.

Exercise Partner

As we will cover more in Chapter 23: Friends, human beings are inherently social creatures. Socializing broadens our understanding of the world and allows us to learn from what we can't experience first hand. Perhaps more importantly though, socializing allows us to express ourselves to others. In the case of exercising, being social also has the power to be the magic bullet many people are looking for; social exercise can be the key to maintaining motivation.

Finding an exercise partner is as easy or as hard as finding a friend who also wants to exercise. When searching for this person, look for the following:

- Someone who is in roughly the same physical shape as you
- Someone who will agree to mutually set workout times
- Someone who is reliable and positive

Finding this person can be a challenge, but for many people finding a partner ends up being the missing component to their otherwise successful workout regimen. My favorite way of getting a friend to exercise with me is by inviting them to partake in a friendly exercise competition.

Exercise Competitions

For many people, the most effective method of initiating a new habit is by modeling the habit as a competition. The associated positive peer pressure, monetary rewards (optional), and social reinforcement of competitions are all tools that can help you to succeed with your goal.

According to Anil Rathi in the Harvard Business Review[28], there are four elements that separate effective competitions from ineffective competitions:

1. Frame the competition around a specific need
2. Break up challenges into manageable, implementable steps
3. Provide resources and internal mentors
4. Draw value from the competition process, not just the results

Imagine you are tasked with starting a steps competition at your job. If you were to implement the aforementioned advice, you would need to frame the competition around a specific need (requirement one). For example, this might be a "steps per day" competition that is specifically designed for people who are already eating healthy but need more exercise.

To satisfy the second requirement, you would need to set individual and attainable step goals. This might be a goal of 10,000 steps per person.

For satisfying the third requirement, you might tell people where they can find the necessary measurement tools (pedometers) and you might introduce them to people who have already been successful with similar competitions. When the competition is done, you could complete the final requirement by holding a group meeting to review the progress of the group.

The requirements listed above admittedly lead to more set up tasks for a competition, but in doing so they also lead to more valuable competitions for each participant.

Qualitative, Not Quantitative Metrics

The key to minimalist health is qualitative metrics, meaning measurements that are centered around how you look or feel rather than numbers on some tool. Minimalists do not prioritize different workout machines or vanity metrics. Instead, a minimalist measures success based off of how they look and feel rather than any particular measurement. The subtraction of extra machines and external numbers enables minimalists to focus on health in their own terms. Human health is extremely complicated and cannot be accurately measured using a singular metric, such as a person's weight. This is where qualitative metrics shine. Determining how you look or feel requires you to combine and average many different mental metrics. To say you feel good is to say that the general average of hundreds of your feelings and sensations are at a level where you like them. This holistic interpretation of health is the goal of minimized health analysis.

But what is the point of being healthy if you can't enjoy your lifestyle with significant others, family, and friends? These three extremely important groups will be the next topics we focus on.

Chapter 23: Friends

You cannot pick your genetic family members. You usually cannot pick your co-workers. You can pick your friends, but it usually does not feel that way. As an adult, most of your friends will be friends by happenstance, meaning they are friends because they have been your friends for a long time. This is itself dictated (and limited) by geographical location, interests, and chance meetings.

In many cases long time friends are great friends, but in some negative cases these relationships just create more commitments and responsibilities for you. If someone constantly sucks energy from you without refilling it in return, you should be critical of their influence on your well-being. Ask yourself, "What is the added value of these friendships?" Unfortunately, with friends that you have known for a while this can be incredibly difficult.

You are the sum of the people around you. They act as the external minds that your thoughts and actions bounce off of and as such are critical in making you either stronger or weaker as a holistic human. Since you probably have very little control over the caliber of people you are forced to be with (co-workers and family), you need to actively audit the friends that you are voluntarily spending your precious time with.

Friendship Auditing

Auditing does not mean eliminating. Humans are social creatures. Solitary confinement (preventing the ability to socialize) is reserved as one of the worst punishments for criminals. Auditing your friends is not about elimination, it is about prioritization.

Completing a friendship audit is easy. Simply keep a log of the amount of hours you spend with people outside of work and family (this does not necessarily need to be tangible or formal). Then take each person on the list and identify how much value or energy they add to your life. (This can be expressed in any way you like as long as you can compare the results.) The following is an example:

Time Spent with Specific People and Their Affect on Me:

Person	Net Affect On Me	Hours Spent/ Month
Megan	+++	80
Sam	+++	3
Mike	+	10
Kim	-	11
James	---	20

Aggregate Impact of Specific People on Me:

Person	Affect	Hours
Megan, Sam, Mike	Postive (+)	93
Kim, James	Negative (-)	31

This technique is not intended to be scientific! It will have a lot of wiggle room and the exact methods and language will vary widely by your worldview. (If you are inclined, you can structure this audit like the Recurring Expenses Spreadsheet as mentioned in Chapter 6: Money. Alternatively, this can be an unstructured series of thoughts and observations. You can make this as formal or informal as you want.)

The goal here is to figure out the proportion of your time that is being spent with people who make you better, relative to the amount of time that you spend with people who make you worse. In order to minimize low value commitments, you must actively avoid those who suck out your energy.

Once you have this information, you can start to re-prioritize. Prioritizing starts with one very important rule, the acquaintance rule.

The Acquaintance Rule

Flat out eliminating a large number of low-value-adding friends from your life is unrealistic for most people. Remember, humans are social creatures. Instead, it is much easier to simply reduce and set limits to the amount of time you spend with those people.

It was this goal that gave birth to the Acquaintance Rule. The Acquaintance Rule is a set limit for how much time per week you spend with low-value adding people (sometimes called acquaintances).

For most, once a week proves to be the most realistic timing. Pick one day a week and start only scheduling social meetings (coffee, beers, meals) with acquaintances on that day. If more than one low value acquaintance wants to meet during the same week, just add more people to the same gathering, as opposed to adding more gatherings. Remember, you are trying to manage your time so that you can maximize the amount of time you spend with the people you care about the most.

I started doing this on Sunday nights at my favorite cafe. Using this system I could avoid the uncomfortable position of having to outright reject invitations, and instead limit my time with them. The biggest surprise for me using this method was that these acquaintances, in high percentages, ended up canceling last minute. This behavior, which would normally have annoyed me, ended up actually freeing up my evening. For those who did show up, we chatted and occasionally this led to better friendships.

Limiting rather than eliminating allows for acquaintanceships to evolve (some might get better), rather than negating the possibility of making more high-value friends.

When to Eliminate Friends

Eliminating friends is never easy and should not be your goal. Unfortunately, sometimes it is necessary. The hardest example of this are friends who are your friends by circumstance (they are currently your friends but only because they have been your friends in the past), and who need to be removed from your life.

In order to be a successful minimalist, you will

need to be a successful trimmer. In these cases, you need to take a hard stand. You should explicitly express your thoughts to the person and actively stop spending your time with them. The easiest way to do this is to focus on the time you spend with your real friends and think less about the time you are not spending with those who subtract from you.

When I did this exercise, I met my value sucking acquaintances at a public cafe and explained to them that their constant last minute canceling and lack of following through of commitments was draining our relationship. I told them it was holding me back and explained that I had other priorities that I needed to attend to. My lowest value acquaintances turned the conversation negative. The ones worth keeping in contact with asked how they could help or what they could do better.

These conversations were frank but they were important. Rather than passive-aggressively falling out of touch, these communications gave the feedback necessary in order for everyone involved to learn and improve. It wasn't easy, but it was necessary in order to allow me to prioritize my time on the things that really mattered to me. It is that topic that is the theme of the next chapter.

Chapter 24: Significant Others

The best way I have ever found to explain the difference between being cheap and being frugal is by how your money saving behavior affects other people.

For example, imagine eating out with friends at a local restaurant. If one of your friends was to stand up from your table and start asking strangers for their half-eaten food, it would be embarrassing for you and your other friends. If however, when trying to save some money your friend simply didn't order a soft drink and instead ordered a water, it would accomplish their goal without any negative impact toward others.

If your efforts isolate you and offend other people, you are being cheap. If your efforts lighten your financial burden without negatively affecting others, you are being frugal.

The same general principle applies to minimalism and your significant other.

The goal of minimalism is not to deplete your life, instead it is to create space and resources so that you can fill your life with what is truly important to you.

This is where the subtle difference between minimalism and subtraction becomes important.

Your efforts to remove things from your life must not cross the subtle line of negatively taking away from the people who are significant in your life. It is one thing to clear your closet (analogous to frugal), but an entirely different thing to remove objects from someone else's closet (analogous to being cheap).

While we can't pick our families, we can generally pick our significant others. Be it boyfriend, girlfriend, husband, wife, or your best friend, your significant other will likely be present at the life-destinations of your minimalism pursuits. But this does not mean they are minimalists themselves. They are however, the ones you want to share your carefully curated lifestyle with.

Remember this: Life is best spent with the people you love that love you back. All of your optimization goals should use this guideline as a compass. There is no greater prize than living life well with wonderful people. Don't confuse your minimalism goals and accidentally subtract your life's most important assets.

Chapter 25: Family

Family is an extremely personal and complicated area of life. Applying minimalism to your family is not nearly as straightforward as applying it to your closet. So what can one do?

Redefining the Importance of Family

Let's look at one of the greatest advantages family members have in each of our lives. Family (by the strict genetic definition) are other people who share the vast majority of our DNA and many times, our formative past experiences. For these reasons, family members can understand and teach us more about ourselves than any other group of people. These shared traits alone make family members worth optimizing your life for.

Whereas the other sections in this book discuss minimizing, this section discusses maximizing. For most people, spending time with family is what you want to maximize time for, not what you want to minimize. Family should occupy some of the space you create in your life through minimalism techniques. If for no other reason, this is because without your older direct family members you would not be alive.

This can mean different things for different people.

For people who already have strong families, this means minimizing non-essential areas of your life so that you can use those newly freed resources with your family.

For people who are working on building a family, this means minimizing past waste to build a more full future.

For those people who come from broken families, minimalism can mean either cutting ties or building new connections either with your genetically related family or with a particular community, friends, and significant others who you can experience life's joys and sorrows with.

Determining which of these paths is right for you

will likely take a life's worth of effort. That said, you can make the process easier on yourself by asking yourself the following questions:

If I became unfathomably rich with both time and money today, what would I spend my new resources on and who would I spend them with?

This question is meant to help you identify your most important priorities. Many people start answering this question with activities (travel the world, pay off all of my debt, buy a dream home). These are great starts but don't yet get into the deeper and more powerful part of this question. The second part of this question (identifying the who rather than the what) is the harder part of this question and for most people it is the more important aspect of the question. Identifying who you want to spend your time with is a big question that can positively influence all the small decisions you make about your time on a day-to-day level. Due to work commitments most of us spend most of our time with colleagues or strangers. But why? Isn't there a better way? This question helps you get started on finding your answer.

If I could only tell each of my family members one last thing, what would it be and why haven't I done this yet?

This question has the same complexity as the last question. The first part of the question helps you identify your real priorities and the second part leads you down a path where you can take action.

When asking myself this question I was surprised, not so much by my answer, but more by the patterns that it revealed. It turned out that the message I wanted to send was similar for dissimilar members of my family. My message for my parents was one of gratitude, but it was also the same message for an extended family member who I didn't like. Likewise, the message for my siblings was one of respect, but counter-intuitively this was also the message I had for relatives who I had never met. Just asking these simple questions answered multiple questions for me. The same can happen for you.

Part Three: Making These Habits Your Habits

Chapter 26: Actions

Having finished Part Two of this book you are now aware of a whole buffet of minimalist habits. You have all the information you need, and now are on the verge of implementing these habits in order to access the Minimalist Mindset.

The next part of this book explains how you can organize these habits to maximize their effectiveness. It breaks habits into four broad areas; actions, repetition, projects, and priorities. Let's get started!

Actions

Actions are the base unit of habits. They are the

individual steps that are generally part of a bigger sequence. Actions are the small activities that make up the bulk of your day.

Start Your Day off Right…the Night Before

By far, the best strategy you can use for maximizing your effectiveness is to prioritize your actions. As you likely already know, not all actions are created equally. They need to be prioritized so that you don't fall into the trap of being busy with endless minutia.

In order to accomplish this, finish each day by prioritizing your actions for the following day. I take my list of tasks to do the next day and mark each of them as either essential or nonessential. In my system, an essential task is a task that either blocks other people, blocks myself, or has a approaching deadline associated with it.

For actions that are essential, I flag them in my system (which turns them orange) and I add them to my to-do list for the following day. For actions that are useful but not essential, I do not flag them, but do add them to my to-do list for the following day.

As a result, I wake up every morning with a prioritized list of what needs to get done that day. As soon as I wake up, I start completing the essential (orange flagged) tasks. If I am able to finish all of these within a given day (which normally is the case), I then move on to the nonessential actions. This means that my days tend to be productive and forward moving.

An Action Must Be Simple

As a base unit, it is imperative that individual actions remain actually individual. For example, when adding a to-do list action to your list, you may be tempted to add something like "call neighbor and discuss overgrown tree." If this is a task that you are dreading, your mind is going to work hard to prevent you from doing this. One of the mind's most utilized tricks is to come up with blockers. In the example before, this may be your mind telling you that you don't actually know the neighbor's phone number, which means you can't complete the task.

In order to overcome the natural hurdles your mind will put in place, you need to break down the hurdles into smaller, easier to overcome, obstacles. Not knowing a necessary phone number is a legitimate excuse, but it is not a true blocker. To override these mental procrastination actions, make sure your actions are actually individual actions.

The item, "Call neighbor and discuss overgrown tree" is not actually an individual action, instead it is a series of actions which is more accurately called a project. (The word "and" is a dead giveaway of this and should always be avoided in written actions.) If you find yourself procrastinating on a difficult action, like the well-intentioned to-do list item mentioned before, break it down further into true individual actions:

1. Find phone number for neighbor
2. Draft rough script of complaints with neighbor
3. Lookup applicable laws for overgrown trees crossing property lines
4. Call neighbor

Avoid Multitasking

Modern societies love the idea of multitasking. The idea goes that by multitasking you can accomplish two or three as many tasks in a day if you simply do them concurrently. The problem is, for the vast majority of people, multitasking simply doesn't work. A 2014 study in the Journal of Experimental Psychology[29] found that interruptions as brief as two seconds were enough to double the number of errors participants made in an assigned task.

Focus is hard enough to maintain as it is. Trying to split focus two or even three ways inevitably dilutes your effectiveness at any given task.

If you are like most people and multitasking is not

for you, acknowledge multitasking is not an effective tool and simply work on one task at a time. In action, that might mean disabling tabs in your browser, disabling non-critical notifications on your mobile phone, or simply working in an office with the door closed.

If multitasking isn't working for you, stop doing it. You can use your unique powers for something else.

Work the Right Way

Like it or not, humans are habitual creatures. We instinctively set daily (although malleable) time blocks for sleeping, eating, and other daily habits. (Sleep is at night, meals happen around the beginning, middle, and end of the day, etc.) However, times are not the only anchor of habits, we also set habits around places.

With smartphones and laptops, it is incredibly easy to work while in your bed. Unfortunately, this habit forms a mental trap. Once you associate your bed with the parts of your brain that allow you to concentrate on work, it becomes very hard to break this association.

At night in your bed, a time and place where you had previously trained yourself to sleep, your brain now associates it with work and you are left unable to get the sleep you need.

Break this habit by making a strict "no working in bed" policy. (One of my editors uses the strict rule that beds are only for sleeping and sex, no exceptions!) Instead of checking your phone while still tucked under the covers, form the habit of moving to what you have declared a "work only location" (maybe a specific chair or home desk) and start your phone-checking there.

Now that the concept of actions are more clear, let's investigate the next step and dive into projects.

Chapter 27: Projects

Projects are any unit of work that requires two or more actions. (This is based off of the framework of *Getting Things Done*, which was developed by David Allen[30].) I use these building blocks to segment out my day. Rather than telling myself I am going to the office or a cafe to work on any given action, I tell myself I am going to a location to work on a specific project. This helps keep me motivated (by keeping my eye on the bigger picture) and helps prevent me from getting overloaded by complicated work days.

The Danger of Project Management over Optimization

There is no project management tool that will complete all of your projects for you. Many people, my past self included, obsess over finding the perfect project management tool rather than doing the actual work that needs to get done. A much better use of your time is to hyper-focus on decreasing the amount of projects that you are currently working on doing the actions required to finish them. If you find yourself in the all too common situation of obsessing over perfecting your project management tool, stop and go do some real work! The first step to decreasing your amount of projects is to set limits.

How to Set Limits

The best project management advice that I have ever received was to limit the amount of on-going projects I tried to do at any given time. My friend, Sam Niccolls, saw me stressed out one day and asked me what I was working on. Exhausted, I rattled off dozens of projects that were currently on my plate. Sam waited for me to finish my crazy list and then gave me the advice I needed to hear. "That is your problem right there! You have too many projects going on right now, you can't possibly make substantial progress on any of them if you have too many projects demanding your attention at any given time!"

This advice turned out to be vital for me. Making the small tweak of limiting how many projects I took on concurrently has made a huge difference in my life. By limiting the amount of projects I work on during a day (remember not at once, as multitasking doesn't work for many people), I can maintain a narrow and dedicated focus while keeping output and quality high. In other words, I am able to maintain a Minimalist Mindset.

After much trial and error, I found that the magic number of projects that I can take on at any given point is six (three personal and three business projects). If I try to take on more projects than that, I find I get overwhelmed and all of my work suffers.

After I found this magic number, I changed my project system.

Now if I am working on six projects and I am assigned a new one, I simply defer a project so that I keep my current workload at six. Deferring a project adds to my backlog but it doesn't detract from my current performance on necessary projects. This way, no project gets dropped and I am able to focus on the projects that currently deserve my limited attention and resources.

(Keep in mind you are still only working on one action at a time. These actions will just likely be split between different projects that are moving at different speeds.)

Your magic number might be different from mine but I am sure you have a limit. By listening to your body and mind you can learn your concurrent project limit and find your optimal balance for output and quality.

Once you have prioritized your actions and found your concurrent project limit, you become ready to take on the next important step, repetition.

Chapter 28: Repetition

The only way actions and projects can become habits is through repetition. This is a scary sounding concept, as the idea of repetition is the stuff of robots, the very antithesis of a life lived well. So how does one turn actions into the habits necessary to maintain the Minimalist Mindset without turning into a robo-sapien?

You Are Your Habits

Habits have the unique ability of becoming how we define and label people.

If you smoke a cigarette one time you are not a

smoker. But if you develop the bad habit of smoking, you become a smoker to everyone who knows of your habit. The action of smoking one cigarette has little impact on your whole life, but the habit of smoking becomes how people categorize and understand you. Once you get identified with that label, it is extremely difficult to remove.

As such, habits are not merely tools for organizing actions, they are tools for how humans classify other humans.

Habits: Out with Old, in with the New

Normally, actions only make small impacts. It takes habits to create an enduring change with massive impact. Luckily, humans are predisposed to creating new habits.

The formula for creating a habit is so simple that you were essentially born knowing it. To create a habit, simply repeat an action many times. If you start with a cue, repeat the pattern enough and end with a consistent reward, your mind (through pattern recognition) and your body (through muscle memory) will internalize the potentially complex action as a single unit (a chunk) and you will no longer need to consciously think about it.

Even though the act of walking is complex (dozens of bones, muscles, and organs working together to propel your body forward while it navigates a constantly changing environment), you likely don't have to consciously think about it. Taking steps has become a habit and your mind handles it while you think about other things.

But if the formula is so simple, why do so many well-intentioned habits never fully stick? The answer has to do with understanding the landscape of your current sets of habits.

In the context of the smoking example, the introduction of a new habit of not smoking will require dismantling many other (potentially quite strong) habits that currently exist. Some of these forces are neural (like the brain reward chemicals that are produced when you smoke), others are social (like the positive conversations you have while on a smoke break), and still others are environmental (like a smoking balcony) that signal to start a habit. The human body is not a blank slate. The introduction of new habits is reliant on the deconstruction of previously held habits. In this case as well as many others, addition is not possible without subtraction.

Starting New Habits

There is not a "one size fits all" plan for implementing habits. While the formula is simple (start with a cue, do the same action or series of actions many times, always end with a reward), the context of previously existing habits is extremely complex and personal. That said, there are different tools that work for different situations. In my experience, the most useful methods for creating new habits are as follows:

The Reward Method

This is the most popular method for creating new habits. The idea is simple. To implement this method, simply reward yourself with something each time you successfully complete the desired action or series of actions. The rewards don't need to be big, a simple piece of candy or a cheerful high five can be enough. A common example of this is people who reward themselves by listening to their favorite song after completing a predetermined amount of steps during the day.

The Shame Method

This method is the exact opposite of the reward method. Rather than rewarding yourself for completing a desired series of actions, this method has you punish or shame yourself for not completing the desired goal. In many cases this method can be more effective than the reward based method, as humans tend to react more strongly to negative social stimuli than they do to positive social stimuli. (e.g., insults tend to hurt more than compliments feel good). A common example of this method is by giving a friend or charity a large sum of money if you do not complete a series of actions daily for a set period of time.

The Discipline Method

For most people, this is the least successful method of the group. This method requires no external stimuli and instead requires you to be strong headed and push your habit into existence. A common example of this is weightlifters who develop habits simply by pushing themselves to work hard every time they go to the gym.

The method that will work best for you will vary depending on which habits you already have in place and how positive and negative stimuli affect you individually. The trick is to experiment and figure out your most successful method.

Habitual Behavior and a Better Future

Habits are powerful and enriching, precisely

because after they are set up, you don't have to focus on them. I think blogger and minimalist Tynan says it best[31]:

> *Yet another amazing thing about habits … is that they become more and more easy to maintain as time passes. When you plant a seed you have to protect it and water it and feed it. Once it becomes a tree, you can leave it alone and it will continue to deepen its roots without any attention from you at all. The same goes for developing habits: at first you have to be hyper vigilant and make sure the habit never gets broken. After a while it fades to the background and becomes integrated with your identity.*

Habits take effort when you are first building them, but inherently what makes them habits also make them elements of your life that don't require your focus. When healthy habits are properly nurtured, they become the building blocks of the best accomplishments of your life. They become the hard working warriors of your internal empire.

Prioritization

In order to prioritize the projects and habits in your life, you need to understand your personal priorities. Just because your boss says a project is important doesn't necessarily mean it is an important project for your well-being. It is extremely easy to get distracted by day-to-day work and lose sight of the things that make you happy. This is why living life well is so hard.

We are constantly inundated with distractions and it is up to each of us individually to decide what is important to us and what is not. This is a daily battle that we will start fighting together in the next part of this book.

Part Four: But Why?

Chapter 29: Why Are You Here?

At this point we have covered many habits that require you to eliminate things from your life. This brings up an extremely important question. Why? Why sacrifice this much? Why engage in this fight? Why would anyone put this much effort into saying no?

These are absolutely the right questions. Very little of what has been described in this book is easy. So why make the required effort?

The answer is highly personal and dependent on your lifestyle and worldview. *Your* answer will start with a simple question.

The benefit of eliminating the extraneous is that doing so frees up your time, money, and energy so that you can pursue the projects that enable you to live life well. Saying no to things that don't ultimately matter sets you up to pursue the things that will let you tell your life story with a beaming smile.

If you haven't already, now is the perfect time to start asking yourself two simple but important questions:

- Why are you here?
- Why do you choose to take breath after breath?

These are deep questions without an easy answer, but taking the time and effort to try to answer these can help you create a measuring stick for prioritizing your life's activities and responsibilities.

When I was struggling with depression and at the lowest point of my life, I asked myself these questions. Initially I got caught up on the complexity of them. I became frustrated that the questions were just too big to answer.

Then, I tried a different angle. I gave an arbitrary answer. I picked something that seemed mostly reasonable (a Life List) and made that the purpose of my life.

Interestingly, it was the act of picking a purpose, not the purpose itself, that radically improved my life.

It was having a direction, not the direction itself, that proved to be important. It gave me the compass and measuring stick that I needed to decide what was important to me and what was not.

Chapter 30: Learning from Those Who Don't Know

Have you ever seen a child discover something new? Maybe it is the rocks that make up a handful of gravel, or maybe it is their first rainbow. The intrinsic beauty isn't important, instead it is the act of discovery that takes precedent. As children explore their new discovery, their faces light up with wonder and excitement. It is as if they are experiencing a whole new universe.

Children have the luxury of inexperience. To them, practically everything is a new experience, a new opportunity to learn.

As adults, we have less new experiences and as

such lose access to the joy that came from new learnings.

Luckily there is a workaround. Travel and adventure bring that feeling of wonder back.

Walking around a grocery store in my hometown is a chore that I endure. Walking around a grocery store in Qatar is a treat! Each new fruit, each new smell, and each new pastry is a new world for me in that moment. The wonder I experienced as a child comes rushing back.

I want to live life well and I know that feat requires a great journey, not just a series of destinations.

That is my answer to why I am here. That is the reason I pursue the Minimalist Mindset.

Addition is not possible without subtraction. You now have exposure to the habits that you need to prioritize the creation of a better life story for yourself.

You finally have access to the Minimalist Mindset. It is now up to you to step out of the Cave.

About the Author

In 2010, Danny Dover assigned a deadline of May 25, 2017, to his life. He was tired of hearing about other people's exciting lives and decided to jump-start his own by taking steps to actually live as if the end was in sight. He tattooed his deadline on his butt and made the sole purpose of his life to complete his Life List (a list of more than 150 life goals). While pursuing his list, he inadvertently became a minimalist in order to gain the necessary focus to create a more meaningful life. This seemingly small change in mindset (which he later detailed in *The Minimalist Mindset*) dramatically changed his life for the better.

As of 2017, Dover has completed his entire Life List (which included living alone in the wilderness for a month, traveling to nearly 100 countries, mountain climbing in Antarctica, becoming a best-selling author with his book *Search Engine Optimization Secrets* and many other adventures). More importantly, though, he has a small group of deep friendships and is able to spend much of his time writing for an extraordinary community (https://www.lifelisted.com), and sharing life-changing experiences with others.

Letter to Reader

Dear Newly Minted Minimalist,

If you are holding a physical copy of this book in your hands, you are now in a perplexing situation. You have glimpsed the Minimalist Mindset but are currently bogged down with extraneous mental and physical weights. The most obvious of these is the book you are holding. If you found value in this book and are ready to start purging your items, consider starting right this very moment.

Take this book and give it to someone who you think will find the information in it valuable. Take action, start now.

Having read this book, you now have all of the tools you need to subtract the unnecessary from your life. Get started! A happier version of you awaits.

Best of luck on your endeavors!

- Danny Dover

Talking to Others about the Minimalist Mindset

If you choose to embrace the Minimalist Mindset, you are very likely to be asked about your choices by your friends, family, and co-workers. The following are the most common questions I receive about minimalism, and the answers that I find to be the most effective and valuable.

What Counts as One Item? Are Socks Two Items or One?

Minimalism is not like accounting. Minimalists use the item count as a guiding tool not an exact tally.

The counting is neither the goal nor is it a hard rule. Instead, the point of counting items is to become aware of the items that affect your life.

When counting items, many Minimalists choose to count one item as anything they buy or receive that comes as one unit. For example, a pair of generic socks is usually sold as a pair, and you can't buy only half the pair. As such, a generic pair of socks is one item. If on the other hand, you buy or receive specialized socks that really are sold individually, that would be two items as they were not sold as one unit.

If you ever find yourself trying to outsmart the counting system by buying multiple items in bulk (for example, 10 pairs of underwear) so that you can count them as one unit, you have started to lose the focus of the Minimalist Mindset. Again, the goal of minimalist is not to achieve a certain number or "score," instead it is to prioritize what is actually important in your life.

How Do You Count Toiletries, Kitchenware, and Other Household Odds and Ends?

The real purpose of minimalism is not just to count *things* (See the previous question and Chapter 4: Addition Isn't Possible Without Subtraction for a full explanation on what the real purpose is).

That said, I do try to minimize my toiletries, kitchenware, consumables, and odds and ends. In fact, just the category label of 'odds and ends' indicates items that are not important. These types of items are usually the first I get rid of during my routine mini-purges. During my first big purge, I donated most of these types of items to friends and charities. This effectively cleared and emptied my previously full drawers and cabinets.

I certainly use core kitchenware, but usually I do not own it. Instead, I make sure that the apartments that I live in are furnished by the owner. This does increase my rent slightly but it means I can travel freely and don't need to worry about generic items that have very little value to me. Remember, you can buy a standard spoon in almost any city in the world.

While it is not part of minimalism, I use the freedom that minimalism gives me to travel frequently. Minimalist principles keep my expenses down and makes moving apartments a single hour chore. When I move into a new apartment, I choose a furnished apartment so that I don't have to worry about the generic items that every apartment needs.

Does Food Count as an Item?

In most cases no. Food is a consumable and if you are actually consuming it, as opposed to storing it in your freezer for years, then there is no need to count food as an item as it is going to disappear very soon.

The major exception to this is stored food.

Excessive canned goods, frozen food items, or prepackaged meals can count as items if they are negatively impacting your freedom. Use your own judgment on these items, but if they are hurting your ability to pursue what is truly important in your life, you likely should purge these items.

Do You Throw Away All of the Gifts You Receive?

The first priority with gifts is to set your expectations early and clearly. While I don't value many tangible things, I do very much value experiences with loved ones. If shared experiences are not an option and someone still insists on giving me a gift, I politely suggest a gift card or cash.

If I receive a tangible gift, I usually graciously thank the person who was kind and caring enough to gift me something. At a later time I photograph it to remember the gesture and then do my best to find someone else who might value the item more than I do. This situation rarely occurs anymore, as the people who care about me all know that I choose to be a minimalist.

Do You Not Think Art Is Valuable?

I think art is incredibly valuable. I also think art can come in many forms. Art like plays, movies, shows, recorded music, live concerts, writing, and stories are all wonderful examples of experience-based art. This is the art that I tend to prefer.

That said, not all valuable art is experience based. Paintings, sculptures, and physical photos are important too. For these items, I tend to appreciate them outside of my home. I enjoy them at museums and with friends at their houses. I certainly don't look down on these very legitimate and valuable forms of art, I just choose not to purchase them for myself.

Do You Hate Materialism?

I don't love it. While there is absolutely nothing wrong with materials, materialism tends to focus on materials in excess. I am not a fan of an excess of anything and as such I am not a fan of materialism. In my life I choose to prioritize other interests.

Isn't Minimalism Impossible If You Have Kids?

While minimalism is absolutely harder to actualize with kids, it is not impossible. Remember, the Minimalist Mindset is about subtracting what is not necessary so that you can add more of what is important to your life. Two key examples of what are important to many people are time and experiences with their children. In fact, some of the most well known and public minimalists have children. One of the original, and certainly one of the most impactful, minimalist bloggers, Leo Babauta, has six children[32]. Joshua Becker of BecomingMinimalist.com has two children[33]. These are just two examples of many. Remember, outside of the developed world billions of people live with minimal belongings and a focus on what is important in their lives.

Feel free to use my answers as a base and expand your answers to whatever feels right to you. Ultimately, the Minimalist Mindset is a personal endeavor and as such, the effect it has on your life and your view of it will be unique to you. If you choose to embrace the Minimalist Mindset, wonderful, but let other people choose their own mindsets. Offer yours as an option but don't push it upon others. People already have enough pressure in their lives as it is.

Endnotes

---

1. "Life List," published March 18, 2011, https://www.lifelisted.com/life-list
2. "Life List Progress," published March 18, 2011, https://www.lifelisted.com/life-list
3. "Powerful Goodness" was Benjamin Franklin's way of referring to God. He was a man of faith but didn't care for the work of most of the preacher's he encountered.
4. "Life at Chartwell," Access Date February 7, 2009 http://www.winstonchurchill.org/i4a/pages/index.cfm?pageid=380 (page discontinued)
5. "Daily Routines," Mason Currey, published March 19, 2013, accessed July 18 2016, http://dailyroutines.typepad.com/daily_routines/
6. You are likely going to see a lot of expenses in these statements and you might not feel great about all of them. This is perfectly normal! When I did this exercise, I saw 15 iTunes purchases of Taylor Swift songs. (T-Swift totally gets me!) That many individual purchases was the equivalent of 3 months of Apple Music, which offers unlimited songs.
7. In this equation 100 is an arbitrary weight.
8. See https://www.lifelisted.com/min under the heading "Financial Resources" for the most up-to-date resource for converting gift cards into cash.
9. "Chase Bank Reviews & Ratings," Access Date July 13, 2016, https://www.nerdwallet.com/banking/banks-credit-

unions/chase

10. "US Inflation Gains in September," US Inflation Calculator, published October 18, 2016, accessed July 13, 2016 http://www.usinflationcalculator.com/inflation/us-inflation-gains-in-september-annual-rate-near-2-year-high/10002085/

11. "Quantifying the Cost of Context Switch," Chuanpeng Li, Chen Ding, and Kai Shen, accessed July 13, 2016, http://www.cs.rochester.edu/u/cli/research/switch.pdf

12. "About Joel," Joel Runyon, published September 11, 2016, accessed November 10, 2016 http://impossiblehq.com/about-joel/

13. "2014 American Community Survey 1-Year Estimates," United States Census Bureau, accessed November 10, 2016, http://factfinder.census.gov/faces/tableservices/jsf/pages/productview.xhtml?pid=ACS_14_1YR_DP03&prodType=table

14. "The True Cost of Commuting," Mr. Money Moustache, published October 6, 2011, accessed November 10, 2016, http://www.mrmoneymustache.com/2011/10/06/the-true-cost-of-commuting/

15. "Long Distance Commuters Get Divorced More Often," Erika Sandow, Umeå University, published May 24, 2011, accessed November 10, 2016, http://www.samfak.umu.se/english/about-the-faculty/news/newsdetailpage/long-distancecommuters-get-divorced-more-often.cid160978

16. "Password Statistics: The Bad, the Worse and the Ugly," Carly Okyle, Entrepreneur, June 3, 2015, accessed July 27, 2016, https://www.entrepreneur.com/article/246902

17. If you don't trust your memory to remember if you have worn something in 12 months, consider turning all of the

clothes you plan on keeping inside-out and only correcting them when you have worn them. This way, when you do this exercise again in the future, you will easily be able to see which clothes you have not worn as they will be inside-out.

18. Many people find it useful to go through their "keep" pile a second time before completing the exercise. After you have sorted your clothes once, you have a much better perspective on what is really worth keeping.

19. "Principles of a Practical and Functional Minimalist Wardrobe," Save. Spend. Splurge., accessed July 14, 2016, http://www.savespendsplurge.com/principles-of-a-practical-minimalist-wardrobe/

20. "The Minimalist Packing List," Danny Dover, Life Listed, published April 24, 2016, accessed July 14, 2016, https://www.lifelisted.com/blog/the-one-packing-list-i-use-for-traveling-anywhere/

21. "Healthy Diet," World Health Organization, updated September 2015, accessed November 28, 2016, http://www.who.int/mediacentre/factsheets/fs394/en/

22. "Water and Nutrition," Centers for Disease Control and Prevention, updated October 5, 2016, accessed November 28, 2016, http://www.cdc.gov/healthywater/drinking/nutrition/

23. "No, You Do Not Have to Drink 8 Glasses of Water a Day," Aaron E. Carroll, New York Times, published August 24, 2015, accessed November 28, 2016, http://www.nytimes.com/2015/08/25/upshot/no-you-do-not-have-to-drink-8-glasses-of-water-a-day.html

24. "Nutrition Calculator," McDonald's Corporation, accessed November 28, 2016, http://

nutrition.mcdonalds.com/getnutrition/nutritionfacts.pdf

25. "Calories Burned in 30 Minutes for People of Three Different Weights," Harvard Health Publications, published July 2004, updated January 27, 2016, accessed November 28, 2016, http://www.health.harvard.edu/diet-and-weight-loss/calories-burned-in-30-minutes-of-leisure-and-routine-activities

26. "Why Walking?," American Heart Association, updated July 26, 2016, accessed November 28, 2016, http://www.heart.org/HEARTORG/HealthyLiving/PhysicalActivity/Walking/WhyWalking_UCM_461770_Article.jsp#.WDx9r3dh1E4

27. "Global Recommendations on Physical Activity for Health," World Health Organization, updated 2011, accessed November 28, 2016, http://www.who.int/dietphysicalactivity/physical-activity-recommendations-18-64years.pdf?ua=1

28. "To Encourage Innovation, Make it a Competition," Anil Rathi, Harvard Business Review, published November 19, 2014, accessed July 26, 2016, https://hbr.org/2014/11/to-encourage-innovation-make-it-a-competition

29. "Momentary Interruptions Can Derail the Train of Thought (Abstract)," Erik M. Altmann, Gregory J. Trafton, David Z. Hambrick, Journal of Experimental Psychology, published February 2014, accessed October 31, 2016, http://psycnet.apa.org/index.cfm?fa=buy.optionToBuy&id=2013-00033-001

30. Amazon Product Page for "Getting Things Done: The Art of Stress Free Productivity," David Allen, published December 31, 2002, accessed October 31, 2016, https://www.amazon.com/Getting-Things-Done-Stress-Free-

Productivity/dp/0142000280

31. "Habits, Leverage, and Trees," Tynan, published Jun 27, 2010, accessed December 19, 2016, http://tynan.com/habits

32. "About Zen Habits," Leo Babauta, Zen Habits, accessed December 19, 2016, https://zenhabits.net/about/

33. "How to Become Minimalist with Children," Joshua Becker, Becoming Minimalist, accessed December 19, 2016, http://www.becomingminimalist.com/how-to-become-minimalist-with-children/

You made it to the end of the book! You can stop reading now. :-p

There is nothing more to see here. You finished the whole book!

If you still need more, check out https://www.lifelisted.com. It isn't in book format but it has plenty more for you to read.

I wish you the best of luck with all of your endeavors!

CPSIA information can be obtained
at www.ICGtesting.com
Printed in the USA
BVHW03*1155230518
517121BV00012B/160/P